11-11-21

D0520553

The Writer
on Her Work

The Writer
on Her Work

Edited and with an introduction by

JANET STERNBURG

W·W·NORTON & COMPANY

New York   London

Published simultaneously in Canada by George J. McLeod Limited, Toronto.
Printed in the United States of America.

First Edition

The Acknowledgments on page 265 are an extension of the copyright page.

The text and display type of this book is Garamond.
The composition and manufacturing are by
The Maple Vail Book Manufacturing Group.
The design is by Andrew Roberts

Library of Congress Cataloging in Publication Data

Main entry under title:

The Writer on her work.

1. Women authors, American—Addresses, essays,
lectures.   I. Sternburg, Janet, Editor.
PS151.W7 1980   810'.9'9287   80-13613
ISBN 0-393-01361-8

W. W. Norton & Company, Inc. 500 Fifth Avenue, New York N.Y. 10110
W. W. Norton & Company Ltd. 25 New Street Square, London EC4A 3NT

1 2 3 4 5 6 7 8 9 0

. . . in a time lacking in truth and certainty and filled with anguish and despair, no woman should be shamefaced in attempting to give back to the world, through her work, a portion of its lost heart.

LOUISE BOGAN

Many thanks are due, and I now gratefully offer them: to the sixteen women who contributed so committedly to this book; to good friends and colleagues for their enthusiasm and wise advice, with special thanks to Wesley Brown, Peggy Daniel, Mary Feldbauer Jansen, Patricia Jones, Steven Millhauser, Pamela Oline, Karen Sacks, Maxine Silverman, and Jean Valentine; to Richard Catalano, for his incisive comments at every stage of this anthology; to Tillie Olsen and the late Ellen Moers for sharing their knowledge and insights; to my two editors, Sherry Huber and Carol Houck Smith, for their valuable help; to Roberta Kent, my agent, for her encouragement and support; to the MacDowell Colony, the Millay Colony, and the Writers Room for giving me time and space; to women writers, past and present, whose example and work have inspired this book.

Contents

JANET STERNBURG

The Writer Herself:
An Introduction

I'm drawn back to a room from my childhood—the back room
of my aunt's apartment. When my parents and I visited, I used
to vanish into that room. My means of escape was the typewriter, an old manual that sat on a desk in the back room. It
belonged to my aunt, but she had long since left it for the
adjoining room, the kitchen. She had once wanted to write,
but as the eldest of a large and troubled first-generation
American family, she had other claims on her energies as well
as proscriptions to contend with: class, gender, and situation
joined to make her feel unworthy of literature.

I now know that I inherited some of her proscriptions, but
the back room at age nine was a place of freedom. There I
could perform that significant act: I could close the door. Cer-

tainly I felt peculiar on leaving the warm and buzzing room of conversation, with its charge of familial love and invasion. But it wasn't the living room I needed: it was the writing room, which now comes back to me with its metal table, its stack of white paper that did not diminish between my visits. I would try my hand at poems; I would also construct elaborate multiple-choice tests. "A child is an artist when, seeing a tree at dusk, she (a) climbs it (b) sketches it (c) goes home and describes it in her notebook." And another (possibly imagined) one: "A child is an artist when, visiting her relatives, she (a) goes down to the street to play (b) talks with her family and becomes a part of them (c) goes into the back room to write."

Oh my. Buried in those self-administered tests were the seeds of what, years later, made me stop writing. Who could possibly respond correctly to so severe an inquisition? Nonetheless, that room was essential to me. I remember sitting at the desk and feeling my excitement start to build; soon I'd touch the typewriter keys, soon I'd be back in my own world. Although I felt strange and isolated, I was beginning to speak, through writing. And if I chose, I could throw out what I'd done that day; there was no obligation to show my words to anyone.

Looking back now, I feel sad at so constrained a sense of freedom, so defensive a stance: retreat behind a closed door. Much later, when I returned to writing after many silent years, I believed that the central act was to open that door, to make writing into something which would not stand in opposition to others. I imagined a room at the heart of a house, and life in its variety flowing in and out. Later still I came to see that I continued to value separation and privacy. I began to realize that once again I'd constructed a test: the true writer either retreats and pays the price of isolation from the human stream or opens the door and pays the price of exposure to too many diverse currents. Now I've come to believe that there is no central act; instead there is a central struggle, ongoing, which is to retain control over the door—to shut it when necessary, open it at other times—and to retain the freedom to give up that control, and experiment with the room as porous. I've also come to believe that my harsh childhood testing was an attempt at self-definition—but one made in isolation, with no knowledge of living writers. In place of a more tempered view that acquaintance could have provided, I substituted the notion of a single criterion for an artist. Working women writers were beyond my ken; so too was the option to choose "all of the above."

But now another childhood room returns, one which was round and radiant. That room was the Mapparium in Boston's Christian Science Monitor Building, which I visited on a Girl Scout expedition when I was seven or eight, and which triggered an early effort at description. I remember the Mapparium as a brilliant conceit of a room. It was made of glass, a complete sphere through which I walked on a glass bridge, an equator bisecting the room. Above me curved a hemisphere of multicolored continents and seas which were lit from outside so that the room had a cathedral-like glow. Below, disquietingly, was another hemisphere.

That room remains with me as an image of wholeness. I wonder now whether its intricate patterns of glass have been altered to conform to the changes the world has undergone since I stood there as a child. I do know that my own intricate patterns have altered with becoming a woman and a writer. As part of that change, I've wanted to know how other women came to write and how they see their lives and their work. And so this book began because I needed to read it.

In 1978, I commissioned essays by novelists, poets, and nonfiction writers. In my letter to each prospective contributor, I asked a number of questions. How did you begin? What are your influences—place, background, family, friends, other writers? What is the texture of your daily life, the necessary choices you've made and continue to make as a woman and an artist? Your speculation about what lies ahead? Most of the essays in this book are a response to that inquiry. I emphasized, however, that in no way did I mean to suggest a questionnaire. Instead, I hoped that the collection would provide the occasion for each author to write an essay that was already in her, ready to be written.

I made several decisions in planning this book. One was to include many different kinds of writers, especially those who have worked in more than one literary form. I also wanted to hear the experiences of writers who come from different backgrounds. I hoped that the collection would celebrate diversity and also suggest what women writers have in common. Another decision was to limit the anthology to American writers. While writings by European, African, and Asian women might reveal startling resonances, women writers are here in profusion and to "go abroad" would scatter the impact of our own experience. I also chose not to include those writers who have already published their own books of autobiographical and literary reflection. Finally, I asked writers who engaged my interest, and in consequence this collection is eclectic. There are, however, many writers I wish were included here. Some are absent because of the limitations of space, others because at the time of my request they were, as Eudora Welty wrote, "working very hard. I am now the writer *at* her work." Some felt that they weren't ready yet to write such an essay, while others came up against a tension between their lives and their work. Rosellen Brown wrote in response: "My writing in its way is almost a defense against the ordinariness and conventionality of my life, and so there's very little I can say *in my own voice* that's of much interest . . . I'm not being self-deprecatory, really, because the great *blank* out of which I feel my writing comes is in fact useful in its way: neutral color, background silence." Often I sensed, and respected, a reluctance to reveal and a connected creative need to keep aspects of the self unknowable.

A woman writer in the future may well feel released from the question of gender and its effect on work, but I believe that the experience of her predecessors will be telling. It has been hard, however, to get a clear view of that experience. Women writers have written about themselves and their work, but sparsely; often the material must be gleaned from memoirs, diaries, letters, fiction, and poetry. Poems, for example, yield instances of the writer on her vocation: Anne Bradstreet in seventeenth-century colonial America wrote poems about the vicissitudes of being a woman writer, as has Emily Dickinson and recently, Adrienne Rich. We have memoirs by May Sarton, Gwendolyn Brooks, Simone de Beauvoir; we have the letters of Virginia Woolf, George Sand, Flannery O'Connor. We have even more oblique sources such as Gertrude Stein's *The Autobiography of Alice B. Toklas.* And certainly there are scholars who are working with the papers of women writers both known and obscure, and finding a fragment here, a passage there, that illuminates the art and situation of that writer and, by possible extension, of other women writers. Nonetheless, a fact remains: we have very little by women that intentionally and directly addresses the subject of their own art.

For that matter, we don't find extensive accounts by artists of either sex until the Romantic attitude stimulated interest

The Writer Herself: An Introduction   xv

in the person and process of the artist. But I believe that the paucity of these accounts by women also testifies to something endemic to the situation of the woman writer: the difficulty of acknowledging that she is a writer. Even now a woman who acknowledges her creative power goes against deep prohibitions. To reveal oneself is to be open to criticism, and women have not been trained to sustain commitment in a hostile critical arena. To acknowledge publicly the satisfaction of serious work, the fact that one is doing it, is to face a host of inherited fears and real dangers: loss even of creative potency, for women have learned to punish self-claims with self-negation. The essays in this book cut across prohibitions: they are about being visible.

The woman writer as we've stereotypically known her has been many things: recluse, sufferer, woman in mauve velvet on a chaise, woman who flees the stifling rooms of her father's house, adventuress, "free" woman of multiple love affairs, paragon of productivity, destroyer of others, more often of herself. The images are all too familiar—away with them. In their place, I suggest we picture a woman (of whatever age) sitting (at a desk, on a bench in the playground, on a bus . . .) with paper in front of her and a pen in her hand. No more. *But no less.* That woman is asking herself questions. They are the questions of all writers—form and craft, value and meaning, relationship and identity. One that reverberates throughout this collection is "How do I come to be here?" Each writer in this book is taking stock; that is, she is making a sort of inventory of what she has, of her means, so as to know what she has to give. Looked at as a whole, the writers in this book give us a new image with which to supplant the old reductive ones. Throughout, they refuse to define themselves into a single formulation. Woman is a writing creature? No—woman is an entire being, capable of embracing many selves, many relations.

I had asked each writer that she allow herself to range freely throughout her own personal, literary, and female landscape. And yet a part of me did expect that these essays would be precisely to the point of my stated inquiry. As the manuscripts arrived, I recognized repeatedly that these are artists writing. One may locate herself within a large historical and social context; another does not. Each writer has approached her subject from her own angle of vision, and the results have often been surprising. Other people, of course, aren't obligated to deliver what one expects. Often they supersede one's expectations or arrive at them from an oblique angle which can, in turn, change the shape of the expectation. And so these essays not only deliberately reflect on the creative process —they also reflect the mystery of the way in which a general idea becomes transformed into something unique and personal.

For me, writing something down was the only road out.

ANNE TYLER

For all the writers in this book, writing is necessary for survival; it is "the road out." That road is wide and long enough to accommodate many travelers; what propels them, though, differs from writer to writer. Maxine Hong Kingston speaks of having to make "trails of words." In her essay, she hopes to join in a collective vision larger than what has conditioned her. Her way to that vision, however, is not by willing it but by surrendering to it. The visions come from the thick growth of all she is and has been; she must find the trail and follow it. Alice Walker sees writing as rescuing her from "the sin and inconvenience of violence"—out of the impotence of being assaulted by conditions that enrage her and into words that release her feelings and help to change those conditions. For Joan Didion, writing is release from the buzz of her mind. Images come to her without explanation and refuse to go away; characters also come unbidden. "I write entirely to find out what I'm thinking, what I'm looking at, what I see and what it means. What I want and what I fear." Like Walker's, Didion's writing is an answer to violence—but here the violence is exclusively inner; not to understand these apparitions might lead to violence against oneself. Mary Gordon sees writing as a way out of inauthenticity; through the practice of her art, she changes from a girl who wanted to please to a woman who writes to preserve the "radical closeness" she values. Susan Griffin says that writing can take her out of despair and into seeing the "physical universe as embodying meaning." For Erica Jong, writing leads her away from voices inside her that say "turn back, you'll die if you venture too far." One metaphor in Jong's essay is exploration: curiosity that propels the venture and willingness to search out the unknown.

When an individual writer tells of her day-to-day struggles, what we're seeing in operation is a person choosing to continue, to grow, to not be silent. She is claiming her original impulse and carrying it forward—knowing that as she does so, she commits herself to change. Sartre once called for "a more conscious artist . . . who, by reflecting on his art, would try to endow it with his condition as a man." Now that quest which was previously arrogated by men is being taken on, with full intent, by women.

I had remembered the hemispheres of the Mapparium as being separated by a glass bridge. Were they instead *joined* by that bridge? In this transitional time, there has been the notion of a world split by gender; that notion, I believe, diminishes everyone. Whether women are relegated to a partial sphere or whether we appropriate it, we lose encompassing meaning. The concerns of women writers speak to the ways in which lives and art continually transform and enrich one another. As women writers bring our perspective to this exchange, we extend beyond ourselves and illuminate new points of convergence.

This collection offers, I believe, an expanded vision of what is central to women writers. Against crippling and mutually exclusive definitions, these essays suggest that multiple choices are possible. Against the fragmentation caused by conflicting demands, they suggest that the various parts of the self can nourish one another. This book stands in relation to a well-documented history of women whose artistic gifts have been damaged by prevailing circumstances. Against the need to justify the worth of our experience—a predicament that produces inauthentic literature and paralysis—women writers are claiming the truths of that experience. Against the silence of the past and of immediate forebears, we are speaking for those who did not speak. Against the fear of stopping, we are trusting in our continuity as artists. Nor is our situation truly solitary; it can be richly populated, as it is here in this book which is, most simply, women writers in each other's company.

JANET STERNBURG
New York City
1980

The Writer
on Her Work

ANNE TYLER

Still Just Writing

While I was painting the downstairs hall I thought of a novel to write. Really I just thought of a character; he more or less wandered into my mind, wearing a beard and a broad-brimmed leather hat. I figured that if I sat down and organized this character on paper, a novel would grow up around him. But it was March and the children's spring vacation began the next day, so I waited.

After spring vacation the children went back to school, but the dog got worms. It was a little complicated at the vet's and I lost a day. By then it was Thursday; Friday is the only day I can buy the groceries, pick up new cedar chips for the gerbils, scrub the bathrooms. I waited till Monday. Still, that left me four good weeks in April to block out the novel.

By May I was ready to start actually writing, but I had to do it in patches. There was the follow-up treatment at the vet, and then a half-day spent trailing the dog with a specimen tin so the lab could be sure the treatment had really worked. There were visits from the washing machine repairman and the Davey tree man, not to mention briefer interruptions by the meter reader, five Jehovah's Witnesses, and two Mormons. People telephoned wanting to sell me permanent light bulbs and waterproof basements. An Iranian cousin of my husband's had a baby; then the cousin's uncle died; then the cousin's mother decided to go home to Iran and needed to know where to buy a black American coat before she left. There *are* no black American coats; don't Americans wear mourning? I told her no, but I checked around at all the department stores anyway because she didn't speak English. Then I wrote chapters one and two. I had planned to work till three-thirty every day, but it was a month of early quittings: once for the children's dental appointment, once for the cat's rabies shot, once for our older daughter's orthopedist, and twice for her gymnastic meets. Sitting on the bleachers in the school gymnasium, I told myself I could always use this in a novel someplace, but I couldn't really picture writing a novel about twenty little girls in leotards trying to walk the length of a wooden beam without falling off. By the time I'd written chapter three, it was Memorial Day and the children were home again.

I knew I shouldn't expect anything from June. School was finished then and camp hadn't yet begun. I put the novel away. I closed down my mind and planted some herbs and played cribbage with the children. Then on the 25th, we drove one child to a sleep-away camp in Virginia and entered the other in a day camp, and I was ready to start work again. First I had to take my car in for repairs and the mechanics lost it, but I didn't get diverted. I sat in the garage on a folding chair while they hunted my car all one afternoon, and I hummed a calming tune and tried to remember what I'd planned to do next in my novel. Or even what the novel was about, for that matter. My character wandered in again in his beard and his broad-brimmed hat. He looked a little pale and knuckly, like someone scrabbling at a cliff edge so as not to fall away entirely.

I had high hopes for July, but it began with a four-day weekend, and on Monday night we had a long-distance call from our daughter's camp in Virginia. She was seriously ill in a Charlottesville hospital. We left our youngest with friends and drove three hours in a torrent of rain. We found our daughter frightened and crying, and another child (the only other child I knew in all of Virginia) equally frightened and crying down in the emergency room with possible appendicitis, so I spent that night alternating between a chair in the pediatric wing and a chair in the emergency room. By morning, it had begun to seem that our daughter's illness was typhoid fever. We loaded her into the car and took her back to Baltimore, where her doctor put her on drugs and prescribed a long bed-rest. She lay in bed six days, looking wretched and calling for fluids and cold cloths. On the seventh day she got up her same old healthy self, and the illness was declared to be not typhoid fever after all but a simple virus, and we shipped her back to Virginia on the evening train. The next day I was free to start writing again but sat, instead, on the couch in my study, staring blankly at the wall.

I could draw some conclusions here about the effect that being a woman/wife/mother has upon my writing, except that I am married to a writer who is also a man/husband/father. He published his first novel while he was a medical student in Iran; then he came to America to finish his training. His writing fell by the wayside, for a long while. You can't be on call in the emergency room for twenty hours and write a novel during the other four. Now he's a child psychiatrist, full-time, and he writes his novels in the odd moments here and there—when he's not preparing a lecture, when he's not on the phone with a patient, when he's not attending classes at the psychoanalytic institute. He writes in Persian, still, in those black-and-white speckled composition books. Sometimes one of the children will interrupt him in English and he will answer in Persian, and they'll say, "What?" and he'll look up blankly, and it seems a sheet has to fall from in front of his eyes before he remembers where he is and switches to English. Often, I wonder what he would be doing now if he didn't have a family to support. He cares deeply about his writing and he's very good at it, but every morning at five-thirty he gets up and puts on a suit and tie and drives in the dark to the hospital. Both of us, in different ways, seem to be hewing our creative time in small, hard chips from our living time.

Occasionally, I take a day off. I go to a friend's house for lunch, or weed the garden, or rearrange the linen closet. I notice that at the end of one of these days, when my husband asks me what I've been doing, I tend to exaggerate any hardships I may have encountered. ("A pickup nearly sideswiped me on Greenspring Avenue. I stood in line an hour just trying to buy the children some flip-flops.") It seems sinful to have lounged around so. Also, it seems sinful that I have more choice than my husband as to whether or not to undertake any given piece of work. I can refuse to do an article if it doesn't appeal to me, refuse to change a short story, refuse to hurry a book any faster than it wants to go—all luxuries. My husband, on the other hand, is forced to rise and go off to that hospital every blessed weekday of his life. *His* luxury is that no one expects him to drop all else for two weeks when a child has chicken pox. The only person who has no luxuries at all, it seems to me, is the woman writer who is the sole support of her children. I often think about how she must manage. I think that if I were in that position, I'd have to find a job involving manual labor. I have spent so long erecting partitions around the part of me that writes—learning how to close the door on it when ordinary life intervenes, how to close the door on ordinary life when it's time to start writing again—that I'm not sure I could fit the two parts of me back together now.

Before we had children I worked in a library. It was a boring job, but I tend to like doing boring things. I would sit on a stool alphabetizing Russian catalogue cards and listening to the other librarians talking around me. It made me think of my adolescence, which was spent listening to the tobacco stringers while I handed tobacco. At night I'd go home from the library and write. I never wrote what the librarians said, exactly, but having those voices in my ears all day helped me summon up my own characters' voices. Then our first baby came along—an insomniac. I quit work and stayed home all day with her and walked her all night. Even if I had found the time to write, I wouldn't have had the insides. I felt drained; too much care and feeling were being drawn out of me. And the only voices I heard now were by appointment—people who came to dinner, or invited us to dinner, and who therefore felt they had to make deliberate conversation. That's one thing writers never have, and I still miss it: the easy-going, on-again-off-again, gossipy murmurs of people working alongside each other all day.

I enjoyed tending infants (though I've much preferred the later ages), but it was hard to be solely, continually in their company and not to be able to write. And I couldn't think of any alternative. I know it must be possible to have a child raised beautifully by a housekeeper, but every such child I've run into has seemed dulled and doesn't use words well. So I figured I'd better stick it out. As it happened, it wasn't that long—five years, from the time our first daughter was born till our second started nursery school and left me with my mornings free. But while I was going through it I thought it would be a lot longer. I couldn't imagine any end to it. I felt that everything I wanted to write was somehow coagulating in my veins and making me fidgety and slow. Then after a while I didn't have anything to write anyhow, but I still had the fidgets. I felt useless, no matter how many diapers I washed or strollers I pushed. The only way I could explain my life to myself was to imagine that I was living in a very small commune. I had spent my childhood in a commune, or what would nowadays be called a commune, and I was used to the idea of division of labor. What we had here, I told myself, was a perfectly sensible arrangement: one member was the liaison with the outside world, bringing in money; another was the caretaker, reading the Little Bear books to the children and repairing the electrical switches. This second member might have less physical freedom, but she had much more freedom to arrange her own work schedule. I must have sat down a dozen times a week and very carefully, consciously thought it all through. Often, I was merely trying to convince myself that I really did pull my own weight.

This Iranian cousin who just had the baby: she sits home now and cries a lot. She was working on her master's degree and is used to being out in the world more. "Never mind," I tell her, "you'll soon be out again. This stage doesn't last long."

"How long?" she asks.

"Oh . . . three years, if you just have the one."

"Three years!"

I can see she's appalled. Her baby is beautiful, very dark and Persian; and what's more, he sleeps—something I've rarely seen a baby do. What I'm trying to say to her (but of course, she'll agree without really hearing me) is that he's worth it. It seems to me that since I've had children, I've grown richer and deeper. They may have slowed down my writing for a while, but when I did write, I had more of a self to speak from. After all, who else in the world do you *have* to love, no matter what? Who else can you absolutely not give up on? My life seems more intricate. Also more dangerous.

After the children started school, I put up the partitions in my mind. I would rush around in the morning braiding their hair, packing their lunches; then the second they were gone I would grow quiet and climb the stairs to my study. Sometimes a child would come home early and I would feel a little tug between the two parts of me; I'd be absent-minded and short-tempered. Then gradually I learned to make the transition more easily. It feels like a sort of string that I tell myself to loosen. When the children come home, I drop the string and close the study door and that's the end of it. It doesn't always work perfectly, of course. There are times when it doesn't work at all: if a child is sick, for instance, I can't possibly drop the children's end of the string, and I've learned not to try. It's easier just to stop writing for a while. Or if they're home but otherwise occupied, I no longer attempt to sneak off to my study to finish that one last page; I know that instantly, as if by magic, assorted little people will be pounding on my door requiring Band-Aids, tetanus shots, and a complete summation of the facts of life.

Last spring, I bought a midget tape recorder to make notes on. I'd noticed that my best ideas came while I was running the vacuum cleaner, but I was always losing them. I thought this little recorder would help. I carried it around in my shirt pocket. But I was ignoring the partitions, is what it was; I was letting one half of my life intrude upon the other. A child would be talking about her day at school and suddenly I'd whip out the tape recorder and tell it, "Get Morgan out of that cocktail party; he's not the type to drink." "Huh?" the child would say. Both halves began to seem ludicrous, unsynchronized. I took the recorder back to Radio Shack.

A few years ago, my parents went to the Gaza Strip to work for the American Friends Service Committee. It was a lifelong dream of my father's to do something with the AFSC as soon as all his children were grown, and he'd been actively preparing for it for years. But almost as soon as they got there, my mother fell ill with a mysterious fever that neither the Arab nor the Israeli hospitals could diagnose. My parents had to come home for her treatment, and since they'd sublet their house in North Carolina, they had to live with us. For four months, they stayed here—but only on a week-to-week basis, not knowing when they were going back, or whether they were going back at all, or how serious my mother's illness was. It was hard for her, of course, but it should have been especially hard in another way for my father, who had simply to hang in suspended animation for four months while my mother was whisked in and out of hospitals. However, I believe he was as pleased with life as he always is. He whistled Mozart and puttered around insulating our windows. He went on long walks collecting firewood. He strolled over to the meetinghouse and gave a talk on the plight of the Arab refugees. "Now that we seem to have a little time," he told my mother, "why not visit the boys?" and during one of her outpatient periods he took her on a gigantic cross-country trip to see all my brothers and any other relatives they happened upon. Then my mother decided she ought to go to a faith healer. (She wouldn't usually do such a thing, but she was desperate.) "Oh. Okay," my father said, and he took her to a faith healer, whistling all the way. And when the faith healer didn't work, my mother said, "I think this is psychosomatic. Let's go back to Gaza." My father said, "Okay," and reserved two seats on the next plane over. The children and I went to see them the following summer: my mother's fever was utterly gone, and my father drove us down the Strip, weaving a little Renault among the tents and camels, cheerfully whistling Mozart.

I hold this entire, rambling set of events in my head at all times, and remind myself of it almost daily. It seems to me that the way my father lives (infinitely adapting, and looking around him with a smile to say, "Oh! So *this* is where I am!") is also the way to slip gracefully through a choppy life of writing novels, plastering the dining room ceiling, and presiding at slumber parties. I have learned, bit by bit, to accept a school snow-closing as an unexpected holiday, an excuse to play seventeen rounds of Parcheesi instead of typing up a short story. When there's a midweek visitation of uncles from Iran (hordes of great, bald, yellow men calling for their glasses of tea, sleeping on guest beds, couches, two armchairs pushed together, and discarded crib mattresses), I have decided that I might as well listen to what they have to say, and work on my novel tomorrow instead. I smile at the uncles out of a kind of clear, swept space inside me. What this takes, of course, is a sense of limitless time, but I'm getting that. My life is beginning to seem unusually long. And there's a danger to it: I could wind up as passive as a piece of wood on a wave. But I try to walk a middle line.

I was standing in the schoolyard waiting for a child when another mother came up to me. "Have you found work yet?" she asked. "Or are you still just writing?"

Now, how am I supposed to answer that?

I could take offense, come to think of it. Maybe the reason I didn't is that I halfway share her attitude. They're *paying* me for this? For just writing down untruthful stories? I'd better look around for more permanent employment. For I do consider writing to be a finite job. I expect that any day now, I will have said all I have to say; I'll have used up all my characters, and then I'll be free to get on with my real life. When I make a note of new ideas on index cards, I imagine I'm clearing out my head, and that soon it will be empty and spacious. I file the cards in a little blue box, and I can picture myself using the final card one day—ah! through at last!—and throwing the blue box away. I'm like a dentist who continually fights tooth decay, working toward the time when he's conquered it altogether and done himself out of a job. But my head keeps loading up again; the little blue box stays crowded and messy. Even when I feel I have no ideas at all, and can't possibly start the next chapter, I have a sense of something still bottled in me, trying to get out.

People have always seemed funny and strange to me, and touching in unexpected ways. I can't shake off a sort of mist of irony that hangs over whatever I see. Probably that's what I'm trying to put across when I write; I may believe that I'm the one person who holds this view of things. And I'm always hurt when a reader says that I choose only bizarre or eccentric people to write about. It's not a matter of choice; it just seems to me that even the most ordinary person, in real life, will turn out to have something unusual at his center. I like to think that I might meet up with one of my past characters at the very next street corner. The odd thing is, sometimes I have. And if I were remotely religious, I'd believe that a little gathering of my characters would be waiting for me in heaven when I died.

"*Then* what happened?" I'd ask them. "How have things worked out, since the last time I saw you?"

I think I was born with the impression that what happened in books was much more reasonable, and interesting, and *real,* in some ways, than what happened in life. I hated childhood, and spent it sitting behind a book waiting for adulthood to arrive. When I ran out of books I made up my own. At night, when I couldn't sleep, I made up stories in the dark. Most of my plots involved girls going west in covered wagons. I was truly furious that I'd been born too late to go west in a covered wagon.

I know a poet who says that in order to be a writer, you have to have had rheumatic fever in your childhood. I've never had rheumatic fever, but I believe that any kind of setting-apart situation will do as well. In my case, it was emerging from that commune—really an experimental Quaker community in the wilderness—and trying to fit into the outside world. I was eleven. I had never used a telephone and could strike a match on the soles of my bare feet. All the children in my new school looked very peculiar to me, and I certainly must have looked peculiar to them. I am still surprised, to this day, to find myself where I am. My life is so streamlined and full of modern conveniences. How did I get here? I have given up hope, by now, of ever losing my sense of distance; in fact, I seem to have come to cherish it. Neither I nor any of my brothers can stand being out among a crowd of people for any length of time at all.

I spent my adolescence planning to be an artist, not a writer. After all, books had to be about major events, and none had ever happened to me. All I knew were tobacco workers, stringing the leaves I handed them and talking up a storm. Then I found a book of Eudora Welty's short stories in the high school library. She was writing about Edna Earle, who was so slow-witted she could sit all day just pondering how the tail of the *C* got through the loop of the *L* on the Coca-Cola sign. Why, I knew Edna Earle. You mean you could *write* about such people? I have always meant to send Eudora Welty a thank-you note, but I imagine she would find it a little strange.

I wanted to go to Swarthmore College, but my parents suggested Duke instead, where I had a full scholarship, because my three brothers were coming along right behind me and it was more important for boys to get a good education than for girls. That was the first and last time that my being female was ever a serious issue. I still don't think it was just, but I can't say it ruined my life. After all, Duke had Reynolds Price, who turned out to be the only person I ever knew who could actually teach writing. It all worked out, in the end.

I believe that for many writers, the hardest time is that dead spot after college (where they're wonder-children, made much of) and before their first published work. Luckily, I didn't notice that part; I was so vague about what I wanted to do that I could hardly chafe at not yet doing it. I went to graduate school in Russian studies; I scrubbed decks on a boat in Maine; I got a job ordering books from the Soviet Union. Writing was something that crept in around the edges. For a while I lived in New York, where I became addicted to riding any kind of train or subway, and while I rode I often felt I was nothing but an enormous eye, taking things in and turning them over and sorting them out. But who would I tell them to, once I'd sorted them? I have never had more than three or four close friends, at any period of my life; and anyway, I don't talk well. I am the kind of person who wakes up at four in the morning and suddenly thinks of what she should have said yesterday at lunch. For me, writing something down was the only road out.

You would think, since I waited so long and so hopefully for adulthood, that it would prove to be a disappointment. Actually, I figure it was worth the wait. I like everything about it but the paperwork—the income tax and protesting the Sears bill and renewing the Triple-A membership. I always did count on having a husband and children, and here they are. I'm surprised to find myself a writer but have fitted it in fairly well, I think. The only real trouble that writing has ever brought me is an occasional sense of being invaded by the outside world. Why do people imagine that writers, having chosen the most private of professions, should be any good at performing in public, or should have the slightest desire to tell their secrets to interviewers from ladies' magazines? I feel I am only holding myself together by being extremely firm and decisive about what I will do and what I will not do. I will write my books and raise the children. Anything else just fritters me away. I know this makes me seem narrow, but in fact, I *am* narrow. I like routine and rituals and I hate leaving home; I have a sense of digging my heels in. I refuse to drive on freeways. I dread our annual vacation. Yet I'm continually prepared for travel: it is physically impossible for me to buy any necessity without buying a travel-sized version as well. I have a little toilet kit, with soap and a nightgown, forever packed and ready to go. How do you explain that?

As the outside world grows less dependable, I keep buttressing my inside world, where people go on meaning well and surprising other people with little touches of grace. There are days when I sink into my novel like a pool and emerge feeling blank and bemused and used up. Then I drift over to the schoolyard, and there's this mother wondering if I'm doing anything halfway useful yet. Am I working? Have I found a job? No, I tell her.

I'm still just writing.

JOAN DIDION

Why I Write

This essay is adapted from a Regents' Lecture delivered at the University of California at Berkeley.

Of course I stole the title for this talk, from George Orwell. One reason I stole it was that I like the sound of the words: Why I Write. There you have three short unambiguous words that share a sound, and the sound they share is this:

I

I

I

In many ways writing is the act of saying *I,* of imposing oneself upon other people, of saying *listen to me, see it my way, change your mind.* It's an aggressive, even a hostile act. You can disguise its aggressiveness all you want with veils of subordinate clauses and qualifiers and tentative subjunctives, with ellipses and evasions—with the whole manner of intimating

17

rather than claiming, of alluding rather than stating—but there's no getting around the fact that setting words on paper is the tactic of a secret bully, an invasion, an imposition of the writer's sensibility on the reader's most private space.

I stole the title not only because the words sounded right but because they seemed to sum up, in a no-nonsense way, all I have to tell you. Like many writers I have only this one "subject," this one "area": the act of writing. I can bring you no reports from any other front. I may have other interests: I am "interested," for example, in marine biology, but I don't flatter myself that you would come out to hear me talk about it. I am not a scholar. I am not in the least an intellectual, which is not to say that when I hear the word "intellectual" I reach for my gun, but only to say that I do not think in abstracts. During the years when I was an undergraduate at Berkeley I tried, with a kind of hopeless late-adolescent energy, to buy some temporary visa into the world of ideas, to forge for myself a mind that could deal with the abstract.

In short I tried to think. I failed. My attention veered inexorably back to the specific, to the tangible, to what was generally considered, by everyone I knew then and for that matter have known since, the peripheral. I would try to contemplate the Hegelian dialectic and would find myself concentrating instead on a flowering pear tree outside my window and the particular way the petals fell on my floor. I would try to read linguistic theory and would find myself wondering instead if the lights were on in the bevatron up the hill. When I say that I was wondering if the lights were on in the bevatron you might immediately suspect, if you deal in ideas at all, that I was registering the bevatron as a political symbol, thinking in shorthand about the military-industrial complex and its role in the university community, but you would be wrong. I was only wondering if the lights were on in the bevatron, and how they looked. A physical fact.

I had trouble graduating from Berkeley, not because of this inability to deal with ideas—I was majoring in English, and I could locate the house-and-garden imagery in *The Portrait of a Lady* as well as the next person, "imagery" being by definition the kind of specific that got my attention—but simply because I had neglected to take a course in Milton. For reasons which now sound baroque I needed a degree by the end of that summer, and the English department finally agreed, if I would come down from Sacramento every Friday and talk about the cosmology of *Paradise Lost,* to certify me proficient in Milton. I did this. Some Fridays I took the Greyhound bus, other Fridays I caught the Southern Pacific's City of San Francisco on the last leg of its transcontinental trip. I can no longer tell you whether Milton put the sun or the earth at the center of his universe in *Paradise Lost,* the central question of at least one century and a topic about which I wrote 10,000 words that summer, but I can still recall the exact rancidity of the butter in the City of San Francisco's dining car, and the way the tinted windows on the Greyhound bus cast the oil refineries around Carquinez Straits into a grayed and obscurely sinister light. In short my attention was always on the periphery, on what I could see and taste and touch, on the butter, and the Greyhound bus. During those years I was traveling on what I knew to be a very shaky passport, forged papers: I knew that I was no legitimate resident in any world of ideas. I knew I couldn't think. All I knew then was what I couldn't do. All I knew then was what I wasn't, and it took me some years to discover what I was.

Which was a writer.

By which I mean not a "good" writer or a "bad" writer but

simply a writer, a person whose most absorbed and passionate hours are spent arranging words on pieces of paper. Had my credentials been in order I would never have become a writer. Had I been blessed with even limited access to my own mind there would have been no reason to write. I write entirely to find out what I'm thinking, what I'm looking at, what I see and what it means. What I want and what I fear. Why did the oil refineries around Carquinez Straits seem sinister to me in the summer of 1956? Why have the night lights in the bevatron burned in my mind for twenty years? *What is going on in these pictures in my mind?*

When I talk about pictures in my mind I am talking, quite specifically, about images that shimmer around the edges. There used to be an illustration in every elementary psychology book showing a cat drawn by a patient in varying stages of schizophrenia. This cat had a shimmer around it. You could see the molecular structure breaking down at the very edges of the cat: the cat became the background and the background the cat, everything interacting, exchanging ions. People on hallucinogens describe the same perception of objects. I'm not a schizophrenic, nor do I take hallucinogens, but certain images do shimmer for me. Look hard enough, and you can't miss the shimmer. It's there. You can't think too much about these pictures that shimmer. You just lie low and let them develop. You stay quiet. You don't talk to many people and you keep your nervous system from shorting out and you try to locate the cat in the shimmer, the grammar in the picture.

Just as I meant "shimmer" literally I mean "grammar" literally. Grammar is a piano I play by ear, since I seem to have been out of school the year the rules were mentioned. All I know about grammar is its infinite power. To shift the structure of a sentence alters the meaning of that sentence, as definitely and inflexibly as the position of a camera alters the meaning of the object photographed. Many people know about camera angles now, but not so many know about sentences. The arrangement of the words matters, and the arrangement you want can be found in the picture in your mind. The picture dictates the arrangement. The picture dictates whether this will be a sentence with or without clauses, a sentence that ends hard or a dying-fall sentence, long or short, active or passive. The picture tells you how to arrange the words and the arrangement of the words tells you, or tells me, what's going on in the picture. *Nota bene:*

It tells you.

You don't tell it.

Let me show you what I mean by pictures in the mind. I began *Play It as It Lays* just as I have begun each of my novels, with no notion of "character" or "plot" or even "incident." I had only two pictures in my mind, more about which later, and a technical intention, which was to write a novel so elliptical and fast that it would be over before you noticed it, a novel so fast that it would scarcely exist on the page at all. About the pictures: the first was of white space. Empty space. This was clearly the picture that dictated the narrative intention of the book—a book in which anything that happened would happen off the page, a "white" book to which the reader would have to bring his or her own bad dreams—and yet this picture told me no "story," suggested no situation. The second picture did. This second picture was of something actually witnessed. A young woman with long hair and a short white halter dress walks through the casino at the Riviera in Las Vegas at one in the morning. She crosses the casino alone and picks up a house telephone. I watch her because I have heard her paged, and recognize her name: she is a minor actress I see around Los Angeles from time to time, in places like Jax and once in a gynecologist's office in the Beverly Hills Clinic, but have never met. I know nothing about her. Who is paging her? Why is she here to be paged? How exactly did she come to this? It was precisely this moment in Las Vegas that made *Play It as It Lays* begin to tell itself to me, but the moment appears in the novel only obliquely, in a chapter which begins:

"Maria made a list of things she would never do. She would never: walk through the Sands or Caesar's alone after midnight. She would never: ball at a party, do S-M unless she wanted to, borrow furs from Abe Lipsey, deal. She would never: carry a Yorkshire in Beverly Hills."

That is the beginning of the chapter and that is also the end of the chapter, which may suggest what I meant by "white space."

I recall having a number of pictures in my mind when I began the novel I just finished, *A Book of Common Prayer*. As a matter of fact one of these pictures was of that bevatron I mentioned, although I would be hard put to tell you a story in which nuclear energy figures. Another was a newspaper photograph or a hijacked 707 burning on the desert in the Middle East. Another was the night view from a room in which I once spent a week with paratyphoid, a hotel room on the Colombian coast. My husband and I seemed to be on the Colombian coast representing the United States of America at a film festival (I recall invoking the name "Jack Valenti" a lot, as if its reiteration could make me well), and it was a bad place to have fever, not only because my indisposition offended our hosts but because every night in this hotel the generator failed. The lights went out. The elevator stopped. My husband would go to the event of the evening and make excuses for me and I would stay alone in this hotel room, in the dark. I remember standing at the window trying to call Bogotá (the telephone seemed to work on the same principle as the generator) and watching the night wind come up and wondering what I was doing eleven degrees off the equator with a fever of 103. The view from that window definitely figures in *A Book of Common Prayer,* as does the burning 707, and yet none of these pictures told me the story I needed.

The picture that did, the picture that shimmered and made these other images coalesce, was the Panama airport at 6 A.M. I was in this airport only once, on a plane to Bogotá that stopped for an hour to refuel, but the way it looked that morning remained superimposed on everything I saw until the day I finished *A Book of Common Prayer.* I lived in that airport for several years. I can still feel the hot air when I step off the plane, can see the heat already rising off the tarmac at 6 A.M. I can feel my skirt damp and wrinkled on my legs. I can feel the asphalt stick to my sandals. I remember the big tail of a Pan American plane floating motionless down at the end of the tarmac. I remember the sound of a slot machine in the waiting room. I could tell you that I remember a particular woman in the airport, an American woman, a *norteamericana,* a thin *norteamericana* about forty who wore a big square emerald in lieu of a wedding ring, but there was no such woman there.

I put this woman in the airport later. I made this woman up, just as I later made up a country to put the airport in, and a family to run the country. This woman in the airport is neither catching a plane nor meeting one. She is ordering tea in the airport coffee shop. In fact she is not simply "ordering" tea but insisting that the water be boiled, in front of her, for twenty minutes. Why is this woman in this airport? Why is she going nowhere, where has she been? Where did she get that big emerald? What derangement, or disassociation, makes her believe that her will to see the water boiled can possibly prevail?

"She had been going to one airport or another for four months, one could see it, looking at the visas on her passport. All those airports where Charlotte Douglas's passport had been stamped would have looked alike. Sometimes the sign on the tower would say "Bienvenidos" and sometimes the sign on the tower would say "Bienvenue," some places were wet and hot and others dry and hot, but at each of these airports the pastel concrete walls would rust and stain and the swamp off the runway would be littered with the fuselages of cannibalized Fairchild F-227's and the water would need boiling.

"I knew why Charlotte went to the airport even if Victor did not.

"I knew about airports."

These lines appear about halfway through *A Book of Common Prayer,* but I wrote them during the second week I worked on the book, long before I had any idea where Charlotte Douglas had been or why she went to airports. Until I wrote these lines I had no character called Victor" in mind: the necessity for mentioning a name, and the name "Victor," occurred to me as I wrote the sentence. *I knew why Charlotte went to the airport* sounded incomplete. *I knew why Charlotte went to the airport even if Victor did not* carried a little more narrative drive. Most important of all, until I wrote these lines I did not know who "I" was, who was telling the story. I had intended until that that the "I" be no more than the voice of the author, a nineteenth-century omniscient narrator. But there it was:

"I knew why Charlotte went to the airport even if Victor did not.

"I knew about airports."

This "I" was the voice of no author in my house. This "I" was someone who not only knew why Charlotte went to the airport but also knew someone called "Victor." Who was Victor? Who was this narrator? Why was this narrator telling me this story? Let me tell you one thing about why writers write: had I known the answer to any of these questions I would never have needed to write a novel.

MARY GORDON

The Parable of the Cave or: In Praise of Watercolors

Once, I was told a story by a famous writer. "I will tell you what women writers are like," he said. The year was 1971. The women's movement had made men nervous; it had made a lot of women write. "Women writers are like a female bear who goes into a cave to hibernate. The male bear shoves a pine cone up her ass, because he knows if she shits all winter, she'll stink up the cave. In the spring, the pressure of all that built-up shit makes her expel the pine cone, and she shits a winter's worth all over the walls of the cave."

That's what women writers are like, said the famous writer.

He told the story with such geniality; he looked as if he were giving me a wonderful gift. I felt I ought to smile; every-

27

one knows there's no bore like a feminist with no sense of humor. I did not write for two months after that. It was the only time in my life I have suffered from writer's block. I should not have smiled. But he was a famous writer and spoke with geniality. And in truth, I did not have the courage for clear rage. There is no seduction like that of being thought a good girl.

Theodore Roethke said that women poets were "stamping a tiny foot against God." I have been told by male but not by female critics that my work was "exquisite, "lovely," "like a watercolor." They, of course, were painting in oils. They were doing the important work. Watercolors are cheap and plentiful; oils are costly: their base must be bought. And the idea is that oil paintings will endure. But what will they endure against? Fire? Flood? Bombs? Earthquake? Their endurance is another illusion: one more foolish bet against nature, or against natural vulnerabilities, one more scheme, like fallout shelters, one more gesture of illusory safety.

There are people in the world who derive no small pleasure from the game of "major" and "minor." They think that no major work can be painted in watercolors. They think, too, that Hemingway writing about boys in the woods is major; Mansfield writing about girls in the house is minor. Exquisite, they will hasten to insist, but minor. These people join up with other bad specters, and I have to work to banish them. Let us pretend these specters are two men, two famous poets, saying, "Your experience is an embarrassment; your experience is insignificant."

I wanted to be a good girl, so I tried to find out whose experience was not embarrassing. The prototype for a writer who was not embarrassing was Henry James. And you see, the two specters said, proffering hope, he wrote about social relationships, but his distance gave them grandeur.

Distance, then, was what I was to strive for. Distance from the body, from the heart, but most of all, distance from the self as writer. I could never understand exactly what they meant or how to do it; it was like trying to follow the directions on a home permanent in 1959.

If Henry James had the refined experience, Conrad had the significant one. The important moral issues were his: men pitted against nature in moments of extremity. There are no important women in Conrad's novel, except for *Victory,* which, the critics tell us, is a romance and an exception. Despite the example of Conrad, it was all right for the young men I knew, according to my specters, to write about the hymens they had broken, the diner waitresses they had seduced. Those experiences were significant. But we were not to write about our broken hearts, about the married men we loved disastrously, about our mothers or our children. Men could write about their fears of dying by exposure in the forest; we could not write about our fears of being suffocated in the kitchen. Our desire to write about these experiences only revealed our shallowness; it was suggested we would, in time, get over it. And write about what? Perhaps we would stop writing.

And so, the specters whispered to me, if you want to write well, if you want us to take you seriously, you must be distant, you must be extreme.

I suppose the specters were not entirely wrong. Some of the literature that has been written since the inception of the women's movement is lacking in style and moral proportion. But so is the work of Mailer, Miller, Burroughs, Ginsberg. Their lack of style and proportion may be called offensive, but not embarrassing. They may be referred to as off the mark, but they will not be called trivial.

And above all I did not wish to be *trivial;* I did not wish to be embarrassing. But I did not want to write like Conrad, and

I did not want to write like Henry James. The writers I wanted to imitate were all women: Charlotte Brontë, Woolf, Mansfield, Bowen, Lessing, Olsen. I discovered that what I loved in writing was not distance but radical closeness; not the violence of the bizarre but the complexity of the quotidian.

I lost my fear of being trivial, but not my fear of being an embarrassment. And so, I wrote my first novel in the third person. No one would publish it. Then a famous woman writer asked why I had written a first-person novel in the third person. She is a woman of abiding common sense, and so I blushed to tell her: "I wanted to sound serious. I didn't want to be embarrassing."

Only her wisdom made me write the novel I meant to. I can say it now: I will probably never read Conrad again; what he writes about simply does not interest me. Henry James I will love always, but it is not for his distance that I love him. The notion that style and detachment are necessary blood brothers is crude and bigoted. It is an intellectual embarrassment.

And I can say it now: I would rather own a Mary Cassatt watercolor than a Velasquez oil.

Here is the good side of being a woman writer: the company of other women writers, dead and living. My writer friends, all women, help me banish the dark specters. So does Katharine Mansfield; so does Christina Rossetti. I feel their closeness to the heart of things; I feel their aptness and their bravery.

I think it is lonelier to be a man writer than a woman writer now, because I do not think that men are as good at being friends to one another as women are. Perhaps, since they have not thought they needed each other's protection, as women have known we have needed each other's, they have not learned the knack of helpful, rich concern which centers on a friend's work. They may be worried, since they see themselves as hewers of wood and slayers of animals, about production, about the kind of achievement that sees its success only in terms of another's failure. They may not be as kind to one another; they may not know how. These are the specters that men now must banish. Our specters may be easier to chase. For the moment. They were not always so.

To this tale there should be an appendix, an explanation. Why was I so susceptible to the bad advice of men? What made me so ready to listen? Where did I acquire my genius for obedience?

I had a charming father. In many crucial ways, he was innocent of sexism, although he may have substituted narcissism in its place. He wanted me to be like him. He was a writer, an unsuccessful writer, and my mother worked as a secretary to support us. Nevertheless he was a writer; he could think of himself as nothing else. He wanted me to be a writer too. I may have been born to be one, which made things easier. He died when I was seven. But even in those years we had together I learned well that I was his child, not my mother's. His mind was exalted, my mother's common. That she could earn the money to support us was only proof of the ordinariness of her nature, an ordinariness to which I was in no way heir. So I was taught to read at three, taught French at six, and taught to despise the world of women, the domestic. I was a docile child. I brought my father great joy, and I learned the pleasures of being a good girl.

And I earned, as a good girl, no mean rewards. Our egos are born delicate. Bestowing pleasure upon a beloved father is much easier than discovering the joys of solitary achievements.

It was easy for me to please my father; and this ease bred in me a desire to please men—a desire for the rewards of a good girl. They are by no means inconsiderable: safety and approval, the warm, incomparable atmosphere created when one pleases a man who has vowed, in his turn, to keep the wolf from the door.

But who is the wolf?

He is strangers. He is the risk of one's own judgments, one's own work.

I have learned in time that I am at least as much my mother's daughter as my father's. Had I been only my mother's daughter it is very possible that I would never have written: I may not have had the confidence required to embark upon a career so valueless in the eyes of the commonsense world. I did what my father wanted; I became a writer. I grew used to giving him the credit. But now I see that I am the *kind* of writer I am because I am my mother's daughter. My father's tastes ran to the metaphysical. My mother taught me to listen to conversations at the dinner table; she taught me to remember jokes.

My subject as a writer has far more to do with family happiness than with the music of the spheres. I don't know what the nature of the universe is, but I have a good ear. What it hears best are daily rhythms, for that is what I value, what I would wish, as a writer to preserve.

My father would have thought this a stubborn predilection for the minor. My mother knows better.

NANCY MILFORD

De Memoria

> . . . the act of recollecting differs from that of remembering,
> not only chronologically, but also in this, that many animals
> have memory, but of all that we are acquainted with, none,
> save man, share in the faculty of recollection. The cause of this
> is that recollection is a mode of inference, and the process is a
> sort of deliberate investigation.

I

I was reading Aristotle on memory and recollection and
dreams the summer I met Mr. Sheppard. I was trying, I think,
to recover from having written my first book, *Zelda*. I felt
adrift from my own generation, for while my friends from Ann
Arbor, Berkeley, and Columbia were founding SDS, occupy-
ing Fayerweather, and doping together, I was sitting alone in
libraries and mental hospitals across the northeast reading and
piecing and shaping the documents that formed the heart of
that book. I was also spending a good deal of my time talking
to those people who had known the Fitzgeralds well. They
were two generations older than I.

I remember sitting with Dos Passos on a park bench across

from the Peabody School of Music in Baltimore, where he often wrote. It was one of those prime fall days when the light is the color of topaz. A shy and courtly man, he was reserved when it came to discussing his own work, or his life, and he rarely looked at me as we spoke. We had been talking for some time about the Fitzgeralds and the Murphys and Hemingway when suddenly he turned to me and, raising his hand as if to shield his eyes from the sun, said, "Don't you believe in love? There is love, you know. There are people, men and women, who love each other against whatever odds, and who continue to." He said this with such vehemence that he knocked the notebook I had been writing in from my hands. But whether he was truly asking it of me, or of himself, or asserting it about the Fitzgeralds I could not tell.

To tell the truth, writing this book had done more than estrange me from my generation. It had given me the conviction that I was bearing witness to a life, to the meaning of a particular past, and that I shared that past. I suppose in a way I did. For I had found that the boundaries of an inquiry are fixed not only by the person one is writing about, or by the persons with whom one speaks, but also by what is carried in the heart of the biographer. I learned there was a complicity between the teller's need to reveal and my own need to hear. For my curiosity was like an appetite; it was my desire to know what Zelda Fitzgerald had felt at a given moment, what she had suffered or shared. I wanted to touch the past as if it were flesh. By the time *Zelda* was published, the photograph of her face on the back of the jacket seemed to me to be my own.

I am forty now and still I kindle to other people's lives. I write about women who were legends in their own time, and the stories of their lives give me access to a shared past I could not do without. It seems to me that these stories lie at the very heart of biography, and that in telling them we forge connections between the past and our own time. Fierce and piercing, they hold fast against the losses of time. But more than that, my old heroines give me signals to my own life. It is not that they provide insulation against the hazards of the present, for I am a woman writing in my own time, which is not theirs. But the charge of the past is ardent: tell me what I need to know to live.

But before publication, when I was done writing, I had sent the Fitzgeralds' daughter my manuscript and waited. She could not bear to read it, she said. She threatened suicide. I didn't know what to do, for I could not have done without what she had given me. She turned upon me as if I had stolen her past, as if I had charmed those stories and those documents from her for my own purposes. And I had, of course. I was writing the story of her mother's life. It did not matter much that that purpose had been clearly stated in letter after letter. And it did not matter to me at all that legally I was as clean as salt. The book was published, and it sold as if it held secrets. I went to the Connecticut shore to read, to write, and to heal. I wanted to be left absolutely alone. All I needed, I thought, was a place to work.

2

As I placed my hand on the doorknob it turned by itself within my grasp. I almost fell into his front hall.

"What do you want?" he shouted at me.

"Mr. Sheppard?" I asked.

"What?"

"Are you Mr. Sheppard?" I said loudly.

"Don't shout at me. Who else'd I be?"

"What?" I said.

"Young lady, you were opening my door, who'd you expect but me? I'm going to be ninety-one on the fourth of July, so there wouldn't be anybody else in my house, would there?"

He stood just inside the dark farmhouse so that I could barely see him. His eyes were the color of his overalls, as washed out as a winter sky, and his fine sparse hair rose like steam above his ears. Watching me watching him, he began to grin.

"Don't you know what that is?" he said, pointing to a horseshoe knocker by his door.

"I did knock, two or three times," I said.

"What is it?"

"It's a horseshoe."

"Nope. Looks like a horseshoe to most people, but it isn't. Look at it again."

It was a black iron crescent with square holes within the raised edge into which nails were fitted.

"You don't know as much as you think you do, do you?" he said, delighted. "It's a pony shoe. She was a large enough pony, which is why you were fooled, part Morgan I believe, but she had a tendency to lame and so I made that shoe for her. See where it's worn there, on the inside? Come on in, if you're going to."

As I followed him into his house, it began to seem more and more like a mistake to have come to this quirky old man, and I wondered whether I should tell him that I wanted the use of his barn for the summer. The cottage I had rented faced the Sound. But I found myself disturbed by the constant slap of the water on the rocks and by the openness of the long view. I wanted to be inland on flat land where I could see ordinary things up close—a pear tree, the line of sea oats where the salt marsh began. He led me into a room that appeared to be unused, for there were only two straight-back chairs in it. One was placed in the center of the room, and the other faced it. Sitting down, he motioned me to the center chair. Our knees almost touched as we sat there, and the room was dim in the failing light of late afternoon. The white of his hair and the blue of his overalls were made luminous in it.

"So you'd like my barn?" he said.

I was genuinely startled and asked him if he read minds. He chuckled and said, "I used to be a great reader in my day, but I don't want to wear you out with my stories." When I didn't say anything, he continued. "My wife, bless her, could never understand it. She'd say, 'Now, Bert, there you are sitting with your nose in a book again. What'll it get you?' And I'd say, 'It'll get me everywhere I haven't been, Alice.'

"But now it's all I can do to finish the evening papers. Then I watch television for an hour or so; I never mind what it is I watch, you know, I just pick a channel and stick with it to pass the time. Sometimes I don't even really watch it, I let it stay on for the sound of talk in the room.

"Would you like a piece?" he said, then as he carefully took a pack of gum out of his pocket, selected a stick, and, refolding the tin foil, fitted it back into the paper wrapper.

It was Black Jack gum, and as he chewed the room was filled with the sweetish aroma of licorice, or maybe it's anise. The smell reminded me of the times when my great-grandfather and I used to sneak it along with Mounds Bars and the tin of Prince Albert out of the top drawer of the buffet and then go downstairs to the basement for a chew before his daughter, my grandmother, found us. "What are you doing down there, Pa?" she'd call out. And we'd let her call a couple of times before he'd answer. "Nothing much, Dottie. Stoking the furnace with Toots along for company." Then I'd sit on his lap by the warmth of the hulking coal furnace, the glowing clinkers as big as dog's heads, and we'd eat as much candy as we pleased out of reach of them all. Later they'd find us together like that, asleep in each other's arms, me having put my fingers into the buttonholes of his wool cardigan so I wouldn't slip off, him with his arms around me, in the dark afternoons of inland Michigan winters.

There came a time during my last year in high school when I would pretend I didn't know him. But even then I knew I was being heartless, refusing to recognize him as he drifted by the school, lost again, having forgotten the name of his street or where his house was. For years he had called me by my mother's or my grandmother's name, but it never bothered me when we were alone together because I knew he was talking to me, I could see it in his eyes. It was just the generations of names that confused him. But I was ashamed to see him with the spittle drooling down his unshaven chin, his filmy eyes leaking in the icy winter air. For years after he'd died I'd suddenly see him crossing a street just beyond hailing distance, his long white head with its skin as pink and clean as a rabbit's is beneath its fur.

"You can have it for as long as you need it," Mr. Sheppard said, watching me intently.

"Are you sure?"

"Wouldn't say it if I wasn't."

"What do you want; what can I offer you for it?"

"Company," he said. "Comfort."

His eyes were not blue, but dark gray the way certain

stones are when wet, and speckled like agates. I felt that tug of curiosity rising in me toward him like attraction. But I didn't want to be drawn into anyone else's life, I wanted my own back intact. He held out the key.

"I meant money," I said.

"I don't need money any more than I need the barn." And with that he stood up and left the room. After a few minutes he called for me to come into the kitchen where he'd put out two fine English teacups. Their deep blue figures flowed into the white porcelain.

"These were Pru's wedding gift to us. Aren't they pretty? She was my wife's elder sister and she had a fine eye for good lasting things." Then he said for me to have a look at the barn and that later, if I liked it, we could figure out the cost. So I took the key.

3

Avoiding Mr. Sheppard wasn't simple. For no matter when I came in the morning he'd be sitting on his back porch either leaning on the shovel he used as a cane, watching the birds eating the grain he'd put out for them, or using it to work among his roses. There were fifty bushes of them planted in beds around the house and barn. "Here," he'd call out to me as I walked with my head down toward the barn. "Just look at this Eminence!" And while the birds nodded at one another and chided, a rose lifted its bud to the sun and loosened.

Mr. Sheppard, who had labeled each bush with its name and date of planting, said they were his remaining pleasure. He watched and tended them as carefully as if they were children. And like children raised from the same soil, he told me, some prosper and some do not. By midsummer most of their gorgeous heads were as large and unruly as lettuces. The

Golden Empress, however, no matter how often he staked her, nor how firmly he tied her to that stake, leaned into the shade of his walnut tree and bloomed begrudgingly. Whereas the Mae West, puckered and tight-budded in July, by August flared into lush flower, the tips of her petals the color of a girl's nipples, the inside creamy and as cool and moist to the touch as skin. On those rare mornings when I successfully gained the barn before he spotted me, I would watch him murmuring among his roses, apologizing to the birds as he knocked their feeders askew.

By the end of August he did not often leave his porch, and against my better judgment I found myself stopping there in the morning with a bag full of fresh yeast doughnuts. After we'd finished the doughnuts he'd talk to me. He always talked about the past. Usually he'd tell me about things he could do or knew about that I didn't, and his stories were pleasant to listen to, soothing like fables. Sometimes he quizzed me. One day, for instance, he'd found a small, curiously shaped sharp instrument hanging in the barn and labeled "boar." Turning it in his hand he asked, "Do you know how to castrate hogs?" Then he told me how. Once he quoted a line of Vergil and asked me what it meant. When I didn't know he told me how he had translated it correctly, but how unfair it had been for him to have worked long hours over his translation. He'd been the only boy in his class and had to work alone, while the girls were all friends and shared their exercises together. He felt this was a complicity of women, as he called it, and it made him early shy and uncertain before what he suspected were their greater gifts.

Mr. Sheppard never asked me anything to which he did not hold the answer, except once.

In October the roses were finished. For three or four days

running I didn't see him on the porch, and although I was reluctant to go inside his house, I missed him. Late one night I could see his television screen glowing in the dark house like a metallic bruise. I decided to go in. I found him with his eyes shut sitting in front of it wrapped in blankets. I said his name, but he didn't move. Leaning toward him I noticed that the skin at his temples and on the inside of his frail wrists was as dry and white as paper, and I could see his pulse. His hearing aid, which was attached to his glasses, was on the floor beside his shovel. I bent closer.

"Do you believe in dreams?" he said, opening his eyes and looking directly into mine.

"You scared me."

"Do you?"

"Why do you ask me these things?"

He covered my hand with his own. "Because I am thinking over and over again . . . my life." Then he shut his eyes while I held his hand in both of mine.

He said he could hardly sleep for remembering. He said it was like floating in memories, and that when he at last fell asleep even this resting had begun to be filled by dreams. It was like throwing a stone out across the water. Once it left his hand he was unable to stop its course. Sometimes what he cast in his mind fled downward into the water, disturbing it, entering it. He thought maybe these dreams were like stones of memory, and he felt their reverberations on the stricken surface of the mind's waters. They cut into him. It was like being severed from life itself. His memories moved fitfully beyond his control until he was dreamed out. "If ever you are," he said, "done with the past." Then he told me his dream.

"When I was a young man, I courted a girl who lived down by the Sound where your cottage is now. I must have asked her to marry me a dozen times or more during the six years I courted her and she would never answer me with a yes or a no.

"The Bay froze one winter and we would take hands crossed at the wrists, or sometimes she would let me take her waist and, daring me, we would glide together out over the pale ice to the edges where the ice turns black. I was agile and quick in those days and she was every bit my equal. But it seemed there was nothing I could do to persuade her to marry me. Although it hurt my pride to admit it, I had lost her. "After a proper length of time I turned to her younger sister, Alice, who was not so quick nor half so pretty as she. We married and in about a year, I had a dream. Her elder sister appeared to me, standing at the foot of our bed. 'Pru,' I said, 'is it you?' She did not say a word. Finally I asked her the one thing I had never had the nerve to ask of her before. 'Why wouldn't you marry me?' And she replied, 'Because I did not love you as I knew my sister did.' I believe that to be true and she did not appear to me again.

"Until the night after my wife died. They were standing together down by the water's edge with their arms around each other's waists. It looked like a scene from a steel engraving I once saw at the library. Pru's face was turned from me, but Alice's was stricken, and she cried out, 'Bertie, Bertie! Did you love her better than you loved me?'

"In all our life together she had never asked. She had never spoken one word about it, and I had never thought, or dared to bring it up. I tried to answer her, but there were no words to speak with in my dream. How could I have loved Pru, that selfish, preening woman, always holding herself beyond arm's reach, always keeping herself, from her sister, from all of us? Pru, with her tiny pierced ears which were as fresh and clean and pink as the inside of a shell.

"But what sort of man was I, am I, that I harbored such ignorance about her, the one, the only one I truly loved?"

4

I saw him rarely after that night, for my family and my work took me back to the city. In the following spring he died. I learned of his death because the check I had given him for his barn was returned to me uncashed by one of his daughters. She said that she'd come to stay with him during his final weeks, and that he'd talked of me often and fondly. He'd died peacefully in his sleep, she said.

HONOR MOORE

My Grandmother
Who Painted

I can see from where I write, on the back porch of an old house, the dark form of a Japanese beetle burrowing, devouring to the heart of a pink-edged white rose. The urge to rescue the bloom taunts my concentration like radio static. Get up, pursue him with digging fingers to the center where the sweet is, pull him from the flower, plunge him into fatal kerosene. The garden is just two feet outside the porch. The rose is the largest this summer, "Garden Party," a cream-colored mauve-edged dress billowing against green. The beetle will eat all the petals, turn the rose to skeletal lace. If I get up, I will putter in the garden all afternoon, and I must work, burrow toward this piece of writing still to move my hand.

I work sitting on the large, wood-framed loggia couch

which belonged to Margarett, my mother's mother, a woman who stopped painting and sculpting after thirty years because, as she put it, "It got too intense." She said it that way at eighty-two, having survived five strokes, manic-depression, divorce, years in and out of sanitariums. "It got too intense," she answers, gravelly rasp rendered nearly incomprehensible by partial paralysis. "I turned to horticulture."

I am thirty-three. I have been a poet ten years. At twenty-two, I turned to psychoanalysis because, as I wrote in a journal: "I'm always afraid I'll turn into a manic-depressive like my grandmother." Winters I live and write in New York, summers in an eccentric white clapboard house in Connecticut, site of my nine rosebushes and small salad garden. My grandmother Margarett was born in 1892 in Boston. Her father was a Sargent, her mother a Hunnewell, daughter of Hollis Horatio Hunnewell, who made a fortune in railroads and copper. Margarett always had gardeners to keep Japanese beetles from eating her pink-edged roses, to keep the lavender and white blossoms of her tree wisteria elegantly weeping, to plant and tend the copper beeches which still stand on the grounds of what was her estate in Prides Crossing, Massachusetts. The resources that supported her gardeners, maids, cook, and chauffeur have thinned in the intervening generation: I can afford the young man who charges six dollars an hour to mow my small lawn, but I do the gardening. Last winter, after losing all but four of thirty lilies because I didn't take time to mulch them against the heaves of winter frost, I decided to limit my flowers to roses, for which I have a passion, and wild daylilies, which require no maintenance. I would not call myself a horticulturalist.

"It got too intense." This is the first and only time in my relationship with Margarett, a friendship that begins and grows in the last seven years of her life, long after she has become bedridden, that we speak of her art. "Too intense." The closest we come to speaking of her manic-depression, the madness I interpret as the inevitable result of conflict between art and female obligation in upper-class, "old-family" Boston. Margarett had no role models. John Singer Sargent, the painter, was a fourth cousin, but from a part of the family from which she was separated by the previous generation's feud over abolition. Her parents were not artists, her father perhaps in rebellion against his father Henry Jackson Sargent, who is mythologized as a husband and father negligent because he wrote poetry, its only issue *Feathers from a Moulting Muse,* published in 1854. Serious art goes against the grain of this milieu; horticulture does not. Knowledge of plants, especially trees, runs strong in Margarett's blood on both sides. Charles Sprague Sargent, the painter's brother, made the Arnold Arboretum a force in American horticulture, inspiring Hollis Hunnewell to plant his "pinetum" whose ancient evergreens still tower, with careful Latin labels, near Lake Waban in Wellesley. When his coveted stand of India hardy azaleas bloomed each spring, Hunnewell put up a huge tent to enclose the bushes, so the assembled, sipping tea and eating cakes, could better drink in the glory of the hot pink blooms.

"I turned to horticulture." Turned. And returned, to childhood, to Grandfather Hunnewell's Wellesley estate, the white pillared mansion, his children and grandchildren in their own houses nearby—an enclave, self-sufficient. Margarett and two Hunnewell girl cousins grow up there together, are tutored by a succession of governesses until each Thanksgiving when all move to Boston townhouses, the children to Boston private schools. The house in Wellesley, where Margarett and four brothers and sisters spent springs and falls, still stands, inhabited by Hunnewells, painted the same soft gray it was eighty years ago, peak-roofed icehouse no longer used but still in good repair. And, down a lane, Hollis Hunnewell's white mansion, inhabited by a cousin in her nineties, still reigns in early Victorian splendor over acres of lawn, rivaled in impressiveness only by a front-yard stand of weeping copper beeches that forms a giant, voluptuous, dark red leafy tent, under which five generations have played hide-and-seek.

But Margarett leaves, leaves in 1910 for Florence, again in 1914 for New York. "She went to Florence an ugly duckling," her lifelong friend declaims seventy-seven years later, passionate octogenarian insistence fleshing out the cliché, "and returned a lovely swan." Not ugly, but certainly plain: posing grinning with the handlebar-moustached captain of the ocean liner. "Sept.–1910–Oct." scribbled below the photo; and with two big-hatted chums on deck chairs, she wears a sailor blouse, hand over giggling mouth—"all busy being silly." Margarett got accepted to the Florentine School by telegraphing, "Please reconsider our marvellous daughter" and signing her parents' names, which surprised no one who knew the girl who at seven threw a ruler at the governess with the harelip and, when asked if she regretted it, replied, "Only that I missed." Two years abroad: photographs of Margarett, awkward, and her schoolmates: Fiesole, Capri, Côte d'Azur, and "London 1911 Coronation Day." And then come the 1914 pictures: a chic young woman, silk draped from handsome delicate shoulders, feathered hat, fur stole. The finishing school has done its work. There is a coming-out party at the Somerset Hotel in Boston, and Margarett is crowded with aspiring partners. A beauty, "lovely swan." And what doesn't show, the young woman artist soon to leave home to study painting, soon to pursue her talent in New York. When manic-depression and drinking become evident in the early 1930s, Margarett's mother cries, "If only we hadn't sent her to Europe!" Repeats this to many people. In her agony.

I can uncover no evidence of overt resistance to Margarett's journey to Florence or her move to New York, but she is the only girl in her family and group of Boston friends to show such independence. One Farmington schoolmate told me that Margarett came to the finishing school in Connecticut pompadoured as conservatively as any Boston girl, and that a roommate's thirty pairs of slippers opened her fourteen-year-old eyes. Margarett does learn about the Florentine School at Farmington, and a Boston friend's mother introduces her to Gutzon Borglum, the sculptor, in whose studio she works her first years in New York. But there is no particular encouragement from her family or sanction from her milieu to become a serious artist. "I don't understand my daughter at all," her mother exclaims to a friend of Margarett's when Margarett returns from Florence, paints her bedroom walls black, and hangs theater posters.

Margarett was unusual for her time. I am not for mine. I have become a writer in an era of advantage for women and am supported in my vocation by lovers, family, friends, colleagues. A community.

> . . . I am not alone as my grandmother
> was who painted, was free and talented and
> who for some M A D reason married, had kids, went mad and
> stopped finishing her paintings at thirty-five . . .

Forty-five actually, but ten years don't matter; what matters is she stopped. No one says I must stop writing to pluck a Japanese beetle from a rose or wash the breakfast dishes, and yet there is a force in me that resists my work, and I connect that force to Margarett. I wrote that poem, "Polemic #1," in 1972, groping to name that resistance:

> This male approval desire filter and its
> attached hook, abbreviated M-A-D filter and hook,
> have driven many women mad . . .

exhorting women artists, my new community

> M A D is the filter through which we're pressed to see ourselves
> if we don't we won't get published, sold, or exhibited—
>   I blame none of us for not challenging it
> except not challenging it may drive us mad . . .

exhorting them and myself to risk expression, responding with expression to my grandmother's life: What made her stop? There is not a day I do not think of Margarett when I sit down to write, her half-finished canvases as viscerally present as if they are my wound, vibrating like the ghost of an amputated limb a heat-sensitive microscope picks up months after its removal.

When Margarett was nine years old, she wrote on the back page of a half-finished journal:

> When thirty am going to have a house & millions of animals. Am going to be a nice cantankerous old maid . . .

When she was nineteen, she broke a four-year engagement and began to study art in earnest. But in 1920, when she was twenty-eight, her father died and her favorite older brother rode his horse into the woods and slit his throat. Shortly after she returned to Boston from New York, she sent a telegram to Shaw McKean, her beau of nine years, which comes down in family lore as "I guess I will marry you."

They stayed married twenty-seven years. "Perhaps the first five," my aunt says in answer to my question, "Were they ever happy?" This aunt is the oldest of Margarett and Shaw's children, born in 1921, her mother's namesake, followed in 1923 by my mother, Jenny, named for Margarett's mother. In 1925, Margarett had twin boys.

"Margarett and Shaw were an incredibly beautiful couple. People would gasp when they walked into a party. Papa played polo. Once in Europe he played polo with the King of Spain!" Every fall they went to Europe, leaving the children with Senny, the governess. There is a 1928 photograph of Margarett, chin resting on her hand, elbow on knee, staring at us, directly but not comfortably. The blue stamp on the back of the photograph reads "Berenice Abbott, Paris, 1928." In Europe, they bought paintings which they hung in the Prides Crossing house. Shaw imported the first Afghan hounds to this country, bred and raised them—they named the estate Prides Hill Kennels. There are scores of photographs, house in the background, Margarett and Shaw, four children at various ages, anywhere from three to a dozen elegantly clipped blond dogs.

"She was not a very cozy mother," my aunt tells me, "We'd visit her at her studio. We wouldn't stay long. She'd be intent on her work." Margarett showed paintings and sculpture in New York every year from 1926 through 1931. It was not just marriage and children that made her stop. There was always the governess, and Shaw was supportive of her art, even began himself to paint. But in the 1930s the balance in her life between marriage, motherhood, career, was thrown. Her mental illness—periods of depression when she drank heavily, followed by manic periods when she did not drink at all—intensified. The marriage grew increasingly unhappy. George Luks, the painter, her mentor and friend, died.

At a conference of women artists and writers late in 1978, fifty years after the Paris photograph, I meet Berenice Abbott, the photographer. I bring a small print, Margarett's staring face. "Do you remember her?" Immediate recognition. "Of course I do! How is she?" "She died last January. Did you know her well?" "I knew her in Paris. Then I lost her. Where did I lose her? Something about a play. She sent me to a play in New York and I didn't like it. I lost her in New York." She asks me what happened to her. "Well," I say, "she stopped painting. She was a manic-depressive. I don't know whether she stopped because she got sick or got sick because she stopped." Immediate response. "She got sick because she stopped. They all did and they didn't know it."

I write about Margarett to find out, concretely, for myself. That silence, that unused canvas, thwarted passion and talent passed down a matrilineage to me. My mother has nine children, survives a near-fatal automobile accident, a nervous breakdown to put herself first, to commit herself to writing. She publishes one book, but in two more years, at fifty, she dies of cancer. Talent. And failure. Failure to hold, failure to focus, failure to hold the focus to the hot place so the transformation can occur, carry you out of self, so what you create may support, steady, nurture, and protect you.

I write to understand this moment: my relief when sitting in my aunt's living room after Margarett has left her eightieth birthday party, my relief that when I defend her evening-long silence—there were toasts to her wit, the beauty of her house, the dynamism of her personality, none to her art, and she did not speak all evening: "She is not selfish, she was driven crazy, . . ." I hesitate, ". . . by the conflict between being an artist and being a wife and mother"—my relief that when I in my late twenties say this, my mother, newly committed to her autonomy, her writing, sitting under one of Margarett's paintings, everyone silent waiting for her to speak, my relief that with fear in her voice, a tremor, she agrees with me, and I see, for the first time, love of her mother in her eyes.

Margarett's art begins eight years before her marriage. When she returns to Boston from Florence in 1912, she starts to study at the Museum of Fine Arts. Summers until the war she goes up to Ogunquit, Maine, to study painting with Charles Woodbury, there meets Gutzon Borglum who was becoming famous for his presidential faces on Mount Rushmore. She moves first to Stamford, Connecticut, then to New York to work with Borglum. Her early work is sculpture. In New York she lives and works in a studio on Fifth Avenue across from the Plaza Hotel. Fanny Brice lives downstairs. She and Margarett are friends, and Fanny spends one night, having argued with Nicky Arnstein, sleeping on the floor of Margarett's apartment. Once Arnstein gives Margarett a shirt, silk with his initials on the pocket, because he feels it's an improvement over her smock. I know more about this shirt (and the day Margarett at Fanny's request spends a morning in Central Park returning to find Nicky gone, arrested—they had not wanted her implicated) than I do about her growth as an artist, or her first one-woman show in New York six years after her marriage.

The first show got very good reviews. "Sculpture and water colors by Margarett Sargent are on view at the Kraushaar Galleries. It is refreshing to find work that is so personal in its expression as this is" (*New York Evening Post,* March 6, 1926). "Margarett Sargent is that rare apparition in the local art world, a stranger coming here wholly unheralded and yet with an astonishing number of things to say for herself in her water-colors and sculptures. Her pictures have the delicacy of Marie Laurencin in color, yet in the case of this Boston artist, it is used for exquisite and unconventional expression. . . . Her head of George Luks is a veritable tour de force in its effect" (*New York City American,* March 14, 1926). George Luks's "open enthusiasm for the work of the gifted Bostonian Margarett Sargent—now known to New Yorkers—is quite disinterested because she is not a follower in any sense . . ." (*New York Telegram*).

Reviews of the Kraushaar shows build in enthusiasm each year until 1931, and late that year the headline of a Boston paper proclaims, "Margarett Sargent Exhibition Popular: Pictures Attract Hundreds at Gloucester." I find no reviews after 1932. I remember her drawing, and my aunt tells me she does not stop until her first stroke in 1965, but she stops exhibiting, and her painting tapers off during the late thirties and early forties. "I think she hated herself for not continuing."

And here the stories of the madness begin. Shaw's brother and his wife arrive for Christmas Eve with their children. Margarett is drunk. "We all went home." This at five in the afternoon. Margarett driving down to Wareham with her brother Harry. At first she is her bright, charming, intelligent self, and then, in a flashing moment, she seems drunk. They arrive at their mother's seashore house. Margarett rushes to the long wood pier, Harry follows. The tide is out. She walks to the end of the pier. "All I want to do is dive in," she says to Harry, who is horrified. Dive in. The tide is out. The rocks glisten, wet. But there is no water. Harry takes her into the house. The rest of the family hears of it from their mother. "If only we hadn't sent her to Europe."

After the five strokes she has in the last thirteen years of her life, Margarett is moved to a high-rise apartment in Boston so she'll be closer to doctors and twenty-four-hour nurses. The apartment has a view of the whole Boston Common, but the curtains are always kept pulled. I arrive one evening for a visit. Wearing a fuchsia satin jacket and makeup as porcelain as I imagine Empress Josephine's to have been, Margarett is sitting up in bed, scrapbooks crammed with yellowed reviews over-flowing onto sheets the color of daffodils, a salmon satin blanket cover. She looks up. "Why I'd forgotten these!" she exclaims, shocked, genuine. I stand there mute in the face of a degree of pain no one, much less a healthy granddaughter fifty-three years younger, can console. I am afraid of physical incapacity and I know it. Since she can hardly make her speech comprehensible, would she understand the questions I might ask? Grandma, why did you stop? When she answers, "It got too intense," why don't I say, "But why else? Was it because of the children? Was it because your marriage was unhappy? Something in your childhood? Grandma, what did it feel like when you began to go crazy? Did you go crazy? Was it craziness or just something in you that needed to be understood and wasn't?"

Margarett's sister-in-law sits, eighty-eight years old, on the window seat overlooking the ocean in the house built by her grandfather, her return to this family place an affirmation of her ease in the life to which she was born, an ease Margarett never had. "She was so clever, one of the funniest people alive! Once at Christmas Eve dinner at my house—I knew but no one else did—Margarett, dressed as a maid, wore a red wig, blacked out three of her teeth, put the most hideous slippers on her feet." She spoke "with a ghastly Irish accent" and kept passing hors d'oeuvres "within an inch of my mother's nose." Mrs. Lee was polite for a while, but Margarett the maid kept jeering, "Have ye had too much to drink, m'um?" Finally Mrs. Lee's indignation overcame her. "If you don't behave, I'm going to tell Mrs. McKean to throw you out!"

And the other outrageous stories.

Once at a party she hired wrestlers for after-dinner entertainment.

Once she greeted two gentlemen guests in the bathroom. She was in the tub, nude, bath water thick with floating gardenias. Someone passed champagne.

For another party she hired special waiters. Someone would ask, "May I have a bit of ice for my drink, please?" and the waiter would go off to return from the pantry struggling with a chunk of uncut ice "practically the size of a boulder!" His companion, an acrobat disguised as a waiter, did pratfalls while passing champagne, not spilling a drop.

Once Margarett ran off to Europe with another man. No one knew of her departure until the children appeared at breakfast. Pinned to each pair of pajamas was a luggage tag scrawled with the name of the person to whom each child should be sent in her absence.

In answer to my question, "Were you and Margarett close?" her sister-in-law shakes her head. "Margarett was too bright for me, just too bright. A terrible waste. She could have been an actor. A writer! A painter!"

An eight-by-ten photograph mounted on an eleven-by-fourteen board. Margarett stands painting. 1931. Large wooden easel. Intent on the canvas. Face blurred, for her whole body moves as she paints, and the photographer from Bachrach has asked her actually to paint. Brush in right hand, palette nearly hidden in the left. Hair pulled back at her neck, sleeves of the knee-length, high-necked smock rolled to the elbow.

A November morning forty-seven years later. I am back at work after weeks of interruption: *Mourning Pictures,* my play about my mother's death, performed in Minneapolis. I am called overprotective because I am offended at the addition of someone else's lyrics, the cutting of the play without my permission. Two days ago there was a reading of my new play: two women in their twenties, their friendship, their search, each for her creative impulse, how that search is deflected again and again before a commitment is made. Forty-seven years later, to keep Margarett at her easel, I write about the woman at her art.

This photograph of Margarett is one of a series of her by Bachrach. The newspaper article that accompanies it: "Society woman turned artist." Headline: "Applies her artistic skill to make her home beautiful. Mrs. McKean's hobbies, modern paintings and old doors." She painted as Margarett Sargent. "Mrs. McKean in private life. . . ." How is the family more private than the woman intent on her canvas? "Mrs. McKean herself—black-haired, blue-eyed, lovely, gentle and questioning—but forceful and courageous on the subject of her work." The woman artist whom no interruption deflects. "Despite her big family and her large household, Mrs. McKean is always worrying about her work. She is unaggressive and gentle in her worry, but she is always thinking about her next painting, about the next thing to be done. And about her house, nothing escapes her notice, so sensitive is she to the beautiful that a drooping flower registers immediately."

In these past months I've moved after separation from a long relationship. Half my belongings are in packing boxes. I learn to let things escape my notice, but it is not easy. If it were not for two deadlines, I would not work. "The urge to rescue the bloom taunts. . . . The garden is just two feet outside. . . ."

In another photo in the Bachrach series, the finished painting sits on the easel. A self-portrait. Yearning, not eagerness in the wide-open, light-blue eyes. And sadness. Nothing gentle unless you can call pain gentle. Margarett's face in the photograph not girl-beautiful as in this self-portrait. Thickening neck. Thickening cheeks. A puffiness, probably from drinking. "As children we didn't really know about the sickness," my aunt tells me. "All we knew was that some mornings we were told we could tiptoe in and kiss our mother, but that she was sleeping late because she was tired. And we would go in, and the shades would be drawn."

I imagine two women in 1931, who, reading the morning *Globe,* might have seen Margarett's photograph and read the article. One has children and no one to care for them, should she want or need just to go to bed and draw the shades. This is a woman whose dreams—to be a painter, a writer, an actress—were put aside when she married at sixteen, had her first baby at seventeen. In the photograph, Margarett stands, uninterrupted, brush raised. A quilt slung over a screen encloses the space where she works in her studio. The other woman I imagine is an artist Margarett's age, single, who works unphotographed, without money, no high-necked smock, no studio. When these women read the article, do they become angry with this woman who is an artist with children, with the money to work as she pleases? Would they realize that Margarett Sargent resents this description of her house at the expense of her work, that this "socialite" is also a serious artist? Would they have sympathy with the difficulty I share with Margarett, learning to work if you don't have to work to earn a living? There is no way either of my imagined women will learn that Margarett Sargent stops painting. But she does stop. Would either of these women, each in her own difficult circumstance, have imagined that something in Margarett's situation would stop her art?

"We would go up and visit her in her studio. She would say hello, but she would be intent on her work." "It got too intense." Too intense. That feeling in me. At the moment of perfection in the work, life is balanced. Then some event, some moment, throws the balance, and I do not work for days, feel what Margarett felt standing at the end of the pier. "She got sick because she stopped. They all did, and they didn't know it." The urge to stop: to call someone, or to eat, or to weep. These interruptions are more staunchly supported inside me than perseverance. The battle is to hold to the vision I know I must express, but the confidence to do it, where does that come from?

"You will have a bosom like your grandmother's," my mother says. I am eleven, standing with her near the brass-fixtured highboy on the second-floor landing of our house in Indianapolis. My mother, black-haired, olive-skinned. My brother teases me for being too pale, too round—"white and gooshy, white and gooshy"—and I reassure myself: I am like my grandmother. She had black hair and very white skin. Like mine. She is not called pale. She is called wonderfully fair.

"I was flat-chested until I had children," my mother says, pulling my first bra from the underwear drawer. "I envy you your bosom." Thirteen. Ever since the blue-plaid straight skirt would not pass my hips that day we shopped in Indianapolis, I call myself fat. Alone in the mirrored dressing room I share with two sisters, I cup new breasts with small, wide hands. Bosom like my grandmother's. The bosom grows. And the buttocks. "What's that behind you?" my mother jokes as we walk together down a midwestern street. Fat. Fat as Margarett's face in the picture she sent from Brittany in 1952. The only picture of her in our house. Framed. A fat face. Too fat for the Breton headdress. Too sad to look at for long. I finger the red felt jacket she sent from Saint-Malo. It lasts. Grandma sent it from France! The fat face. Whimsy of the red jacket. She taught me to draw. To want to write letters in strange colored inks on unusual paper.

It could have been any day in the years before the truce my mother and I reached when I left home. It happened a lot in the years my bosom was becoming like my grandmother's. Standing in the twenties vintage maroon bathroom so the other children wouldn't hear, my mother and I scream at each other for "reasons" having to do with hair—"Sweetie, keep it away from your face!" And she pushes it from my face. And I yank her hand away. And there is silence, then, "There, that's lovely," the side of my face revealed when the hair goes behind the ear. Bitch. Under my breath. Messy room. A slap. My face. Not often. Punctuation to the fights with my mother. Not fights. One long fight. She is cool. I am not. Margarett's fat face. Too sad to look at for long. My mother dead now. I am left with reports of witnesses, war correspondents. "All the time," my brother says. "Screaming at you. Screaming." And my sister. "Once I asked Mom, why are you so mean to Honor?" "What did she say?" "Nothing." And my father. "My psychiatrist told me to stay out of it: mothers and daughters. . . ." My brother twenty years later: "She was fighting something back in you. Definitely. Tamping it down. It was her mother in you. She saw Margarett growing in you."

"Grandma was selfish," my mother says. "She and Papa fought. Terrible being at home. Away as much as I could be." And my aunt: "Jenny and I tried to talk Papa into leaving her sooner, getting a divorce. But he said he couldn't leave us with her. Nearly impossible in those days for fathers to get custody." So he waited to divorce her until the children grew up, we grandchildren were told. As if it was a civilized agreement. "Your grandparents don't get along, so . . ." Nothing about pain, her shock at his announcement. "I don't think she ever thought he would leave her," his brother's wife tells me. There are those who say she didn't love him. There are those who say she never loved anyone else.

My mother on the telephone when telephones were black. She hangs up: "Grandma's in the hospital again." "What's wrong with her?" Mentally ill." My mother standing there touching her head. "It means her mind is sick." Her brain? The feeling inside my own head. Nothing in my mother's voice telling me her fear. Fifteen years later. A white telephone. My mother telling me she herself is going into a sanitarium, "depressed," Margarett's sad face. Oh, yes, her brain. Fat. Her mind. Oh, yes, kernel of pain in my own head. Yes, I understand. That feeling starting to hurt. No words for it.

My mother is giving a dinner party. I help. From the high cupboard we bring down white china cupids holding luscious fake grapes, gift from Margarett, to decorate the long dining room table, Margarett's wedding present. "You know the story of this," my mother says as we place the silver and the red goblets. "She promised it as a wedding present, then she had more shock treatments, and when we went to claim it, she wouldn't give it to us! Shock treatments made her forget even our wedding!" My mother talks in a perfectly normal voice. "Finally we got it, but the whole thing was *just* awful."

My mother wants to keep me from going to Radcliffe. "I

don't want you to have to cope with Mama." Cambridge is just an hour from Prides Crossing. Of course I want to go nowhere but Radcliffe. The time comes, Margarett is in a sanitarium, I go there. Brick Cambridge. Old trees. At Radcliffe I am a midwestern immigrant even though all the men in my mother's family have gone to Harvard for generations, even though Radcliffe was founded in 1879 by my mother's great-grandmother. I cry from fear the night before my first exam. *King Lear* seems written in an alien language. I am too ashamed ever to speak the wish: I want to write. My cover is the theater. I audition, voice failing when I must speak. Work backstage. Skate a surface, the dark water of possible creativity well below, frozen from me. Unspoken, even unthought is the fear: If I thaw, plunge will I go mad? You look just like Margarett! Crazy like my grandmother?

Crazy is not romantic for me in spite of the romance of tortured female madness as creativity, Sylvia Plath et al. Crazy fighting with my mother. Crazy after crying—the feeling no one can comfort. Crazy Margarett, the woman always described as startlingly beautiful, bestially fat, stuffed into high heels, still attempting chic. Crazy. Scent of her perfume cut with heavy, nausea smell. Image of my mother on the phone, the news again and again of Margarett drunk, manic, sent, for a few weeks, to this or that sanitarium. I see her once with my parents in the room she has taken at the Gladstone Hotel during a New York visit. She doesn't talk much, look at us much, fiddles with gladioli in a vase, and afterward, my mother on the phone, "Mama was in terrible shape—" something about drinking, but I don't remember Margarett's drinking, just her very long, very dark red, very shiny fingernails.

At seventeen I do not want to be fat, but I want to love to drink the way she does, to laugh the way she does. I do not want to be crazy, and yet I love this grandmother. Everything she does, she does with taste so original its sensuality is palpable: letters written in brown ink on butcher's paper; a green satin purse with cream satin lining, a Christmas present for the granddaughter she barely knows; the feathery sketches she does of children; the extravagant love she expresses in the arched, rising vowels of a North Shore accent—"Dahling, I *adore* you."

That week at Grandma's wrecked my life," I say. My father laughs. "We were all so worried, but you had a great time." Wrecked my life. What mystery, what example, what illusion, what ultimate would have formed the yearning of my imagination had I not, at the age of four, visited that grandmother in that house?

That house. A dark saltbox bought by my grandfather while he was still at Harvard. Built in 1630. Lived in first by the king's tax collector for the Massachusetts Bay Colony, then during the Revolution by General Burgoyne. Added onto by Margarett and Shaw after their marriage. Old part left intact, restored, then whole wings built so that it becomes, to a small girl's eye, a castle. Entrance hall first Margarett's studio, then, with later additions, a mammoth living room. Tower room off one corner, octagonal, walled with mirrors Margarett left outdoors for a winter to weather their silver to an appropriate cloudiness. Furniture that looks exotic, extreme versions of many styles. Spanish. Louis XIV. Arcane Americana. Copies so skillfully made it doesn't matter that they're copies. Dark clapboard. Pool surrounded by trimmed boxtree. Entrance hidden so the hedge seems a maze. Apple trees like candelabra, espaliered against the house. Windows crisscross leaded, tiny handblown panes.

I remember the dress with the lace collar. The photographs are black and white, but my dress was purple, the collar wide like a clown's. I am small, my hair pulled back from my face with barrettes. I sit below George Luks's portrait of my mother at four dressed as a Spanish infanta. My grandmother directs as the photographer, a small, wiry man who says little, positions me. I stand below the portrait. My child face. My child mother's painted grin. Flash. The photographer changes the plate in the old-fashioned camera. I turn and look up at my mother. In the photograph my small body twisting, the back of my head. My mother, tiny in a brocade gown, mischievous. Not the serious mother I know who always carried a baby—my brother, my sister—on her hip.

We move down the long tile corridor to Grandma's Spanish bedroom. I sit pasting paper, intent. Grandma looks on. Flash. I ride a tiny antique rocking horse. On the wall above the mantle behind me, the di Chirico, two stallions rampant, creamy manes lifted by desert wind, creamy tails streaming to the ground. Nearby sits Grandma, pen in hand, sketchpad on knee. Flash. Outdoors, arm around the neck of one of the Labradors she sculpted early at Stamford with Borglum. My little gray hat makes my head round as the stone dog's. I become part of the landscape of that house.

That house. I remember running down the long hall. Pink. Windows onto the garden, the pool. I remember sleeping in a pink room. I remember hurrying down narrow, winding back stairs to a kitchen. I remember a kind cook with a long gray braid. I remember a man, plaster on his trousers, stumbling through a door onto the loggia from I didn't know where and I knew not to ask. "There was always some parasite artist or other staying with Margarett after the divorce. Some were nice. Some were simply *awful*." Grandma sitting near my

bed. Navy blue suit. Tight black pumps. Sketching me as I
fall asleep. When I wake from the nap, she is gone. I remember Jack, the green macaw, screaming "Margarett!!!"
over and over. "Maaaggrrett. Marrggrrett!" And the darkened
bedroom. "Shhhh. Quiet," the cook says. "Your grandmother
up late, sleeping." I remember shafts of sun coming through
skylights breaking the gloom of the living room. The quiet.
But I don't remember my grandmother's voice. Or what she
sketched. I don't think I ever saw the drawing.

To write Margarett "I want one you painted" takes until I have
my first apartment. My letter to her says something about lots
of blank white walls. Tentative because I have seen only one
drawing of hers, never a painting. Tentative because I know
she stopped and don't know how many paintings there are, if
any. *The Blue Girl,* its arrival announced weeks before by a
note scrawled in pink on hot turquoise stationery, comes
crated. I unwind thirty gleaming screws. "It has a wonderful
Spanish frame," she writes. Unwind, place the screws, one by
one, in an ashtray, lift the lid, whiff of wood, fresh, peel back
the cardboard: yes, the old frame and dazed black eyes staring
as if interrupted. A stranger, huge black hat's shadows smudge
the white forehead, lips set, red, disturbed. Color. Color.
Light blue collars a pale neck, behind writhe thick green
vines, exploding ultramarine blooms. Brown hair to the
shoulder she sits, volcanic, holds the graceful white arm of an
orange chair with both hands, as if to hold her to the canvas. I
am twenty-one. This is my first adult intimacy with a woman
who has given up.
    "Who is she?" I ask Margarett later. Her voice is already
muffled by the first paralytic stroke. "A model." Of despair.

My Grandmother Who Painted   65

Hands badly articulated. After the stroke, Margarett's hands shake too much to draw, *The Blue Girl*'s hands, painted in 1929, splay like fans, prophetic.

Intense color. By "too intense," Margarett, what do you mean? Too hot? The hot color blooming, blooming across canvas after canvas, gets hotter, hotter, then too hot for any brush and explodes, burns out, leaving just a tiny pile of ash? "Who did that frightening painting?" A visitor asks. I am twenty-one. "My crazy grandmother," I laugh, knowing that at night when I sit down at my blue typewriter I won't be able to dismiss her piercing disturbance as I type, fingers splaying across the keyboard, drumming, drumming to tame, to come to know that countenance, the steady acidic gaze that follows me everywhere in the room watching, communicating some warning I cannot yet hear.

But those drummings begin my writing. First inchoate raging and need, then, finally, poems, prose. The earliest readable piece begins: "In the pouring rain one day I drive my friend Jonathan out to see Grandma at her house. She has not lived there for years, but she has recovered enough from three strokes to go 'out to the country' several mornings a week. We drive through torrents to the house. Grandma has not yet arrived. I push open the huge door. The long entrance hall, living room bereft of paintings and furniture except for a few huge hard-to-move pieces. A rose brocade, outsized altar piece which Grandma bought once at an auction in Spain, still hangs at the end of the room, maintaining its handsome shape but well past beginning to crumble. Jack, her green macaw, is long dead, but because of the storm, I think I hear him screaming "MMmmaaaaaggrrett" from somewhere upstairs."

That visit to her house is my first since childhood. Margarett comes, escorted by her lawyer. By this time this lawyer and my aunt are her legal guardians. The windows of the long black limousine are fogged. "Hello, dahling, you've arrived," she says, ignoring her weight, crippled body, the grossness of her face. She is dressed in hot pink jersey, perfectly made up. Lawyer and chauffeur begin to lift her into the wheelchair, she grasps for her cane, diamonds glinting in the car's overhead light, perfume wafting the air. "Be careful!" she yelps, snaps, continuing to smile at Jonathan and me. "Your aunt called and begged me not to go out in the storm, but I told her you were coming and that I wouldn't miss it for the world." We wheel her into the house, and when we are settled in the cold, dark living room, Jonathan says, "This house is beautiful. It's the most beautiful house I've ever seen." And she answers, "This house is me. I devoted my life to it, and now I come out here and keep up the work on the grounds, the planting, the trees." The copper beech, gigantic, swaying in the storm. The wisteria unrecognizable without blooms.

It is on this visit that I see the paintings, by some fluke brought in from the studio on the hill before the fire. The paintings saved, and all her sculpture burned. The pile of ash. In the dark room the paintings. I have seen only *The Blue Girl,* don't know how many she did before she stopped, have no conception. Paintings in a room off the living room. Canvas after canvas after canvas stacked against the walls. Too many to look at. Eyes. Wide open eyes. Color. Two little girls in red woolen caps. Margie. Jenny. One of her twins, my Uncle Harry, a little boy, recognizable around the eyes. A child on her side stretched out on a pink chaise longue, green plaid dress, reading. Still life with cyclamen and clock. A cloche-hatted woman winking, the word "whoopee" dashed across the canvas. Women with tortured eyes, half-finished hands. Women with finished hands. Three children on a green ground, backs to us, wandering in some dream game of hide-and-seek. A man in a tux. The intense dark boy in the golden chair. Too many to see. Hundreds. Stacked in layers against the wall. A body of work. And for the first time Margarett is more than an inspiration. For the first time she is an example. "Why did I ever stop?" The asking voice. "For years I worked. Hard. And then it got too intense. I turned to horticulture."

"Still a worthy cage, ladies and gentlemen. Let's start this fine antique cage at twenty-five, ladies and gentlemen." The bullet rhythm of the auctioneer's voice. Festive green and white tent set up on the lawn near where the stone Labradors, long gone to my aunt's house, once stood. The box hedge overgrown, the pool drained. Tent crowded with people on folding chairs, standing, craning, peering at each piece that comes up. "Refreshments for sale, ladies and gentlemen. Luncheon." A table near the wisteria. Cars surround the copper beech. "And who will start this important, no this magnificent Shaker table at $800, ladies and gentlemen?" And Margarett no longer visits. She has been in a nursing home twenty miles from here for six months. "I hope she doesn't know about this. It's tragic," a woman in a flowered dress says to her companion. And she doesn't know that the house has been sold to a developer who has promised to preserve at least the original saltbox, or that the furniture, dishes, rugs, mirrored fixtures from the art deco bathroom, and everything her children didn't take, that didn't rot, is being auctioned off this sunny summer day, two weeks before her eighty-fifth birthday. I see Margarett's sister-in-law across the crowd, and one of Shaw's sons from his second marriage buys a silver tray. A small Queen Anne wing chair is hoisted to the front and quickly sold. "Aren't they divine!" the lady in the flowered dress says about the Spanish beds from the di Chirico bedroom. "Everything she had was good! Margarett had a great eye."

Her blue eyes, still like lakes. Skinny, shriveled back to her bones, hair no longer dyed, no makeup. Vulnerable as a child, she lies on her side on a hospital bed. "Hello, Grandma," I say, hating that I speak as if to a child to this woman who has lived eighty-five years. "Oh, hello, dahling," her voice is very low. "Hello. Hello." She's been repeating things since she came here. A new drug? Oakwood, mansion turned nursing home, on a bluff overlooking the ocean. "How are you?" "Not very well. Not very well." It is August. There are five photographs of my mother in the bare but spacious room, one of me. Beside her bed is a copy of the anthology I've edited, my first book, new plays by women. I'd sent a first copy to her four months ago. A week later had come her call: "I read your book, read your book, read your book. I've read it twice. Twice. Wonderful. Wonderful." The nurse, worrying I haven't understood, says before hanging up, "When she finishes reading it, she begins all over again." The book of plays about women, each play about a woman struggling to be autonomous. Margarett's greatest compliment to me is the book lying there, the only book beside her in this barren room with a view of the ocean, blue on this sparkling day. "I love you," I say, "love you, love you, love you," repeating like her, biting my tongue not to thank her for the things of hers I've bought at the auction. I am not speaking the truth and it is the last time I see her. New Year's Day I telephone. "I love you so much. So much. So much," she repeats, voice barely audible. "How are you?" I ask. "The same. The same. The same. The same," voice fading with each repetition. She dies three weeks later. Months afterward I ask for her copy of my book, and it arrives, dog-eared, tattered, fattened by repeated readings, in a legal envelope. My inscription reads, "For Grandma, with intense love and great thanks for her example."

MICHELE MURRAY

Creating Oneself
from Scratch

These selections have been culled from Michele Murray's personal journals which cover the period from 1950 to her death in 1974, at the age of forty-one.

December 31, 1954

There is so much I want to say to round the year off while I sit in a train next to Jim riding up to Schenectady for New Year's Eve, but so little of anything I write would even touch things as they are that I hesitate to say a word. For, first of all, I do not even recognize myself, the person I've been all my life, the person I was last New Year's Eve, and different parts of me have been chopped off into different relations. I am a teacher, a fiancée, in addition to being a daughter, a granddaughter, cousin, and friend. And perhaps by next December 31 I'll be a mother, a published writer. But all of these views of me are only partial.

June 17, 1955

It is amazing how much more I can do when I have only limited time—I should really accomplish a lot this summer, since I will be so busy. This is good for me, since I face a busy future, growing more and more hectic every year until I am 45 at least. It is only 3 o'clock now, and I didn't begin working until almost 9 this morning. But in 6 hours I have: cleaned up the house and the dishes, ironed, read two magazines and reread Ezra Pound's *ABC of Reading,* baked corn muffins and blueberry muffins, written a long and a short letter and spent more than an hour on my embroidery, finishing all of it except the hemming, which I will do tonight. I have also had time to think while my hands were busy and, in addition to thinking about poetry, I also worked on two ideas I think exciting enough to put down in detail elsewhere.

October 10, 1955

Couldn't sleep last night, so stayed home today to catch up on my rest and do indeed feel much better. In a very few weeks I'll be able to have three weeks of rest before our baby, like Macbeth, banishes sleep altogether. But I feel best because of a pleasant surprise that came our way via the mail—*Mademoiselle* magazine will pay me $20 for the use of a few paragraphs from an answer I sent them to an article they printed on "The Marriage Trap." Of course, I keep thinking—if only I had done a better job and they had used more, how handy the money would be—but even this totally unexpected $20 will be a godsend to cover a multitude of small, necessary shopping expenses. And my name will be in the magazine, even though it is attached, to be sure, only to a published bit of opinion and not, as someday, to a poem.

November 1, 1955

My love for Jim, our coming baby and my writing fill my life more and more now, until it seems full to overflowing with promise and happiness. I have been granted tremendous gifts, and I *do* feel I must use them or suffer.

March 12, 1956

Another strand [of the crisis she was experiencing] is, of course, my growing commitment to writing as the desperately serious occupation that it is, with all the resultant labor and readjustment of personality and goals.

And along with that commitment is the corollary abandonment of plans and dreams held for so many years they had become a part of my life. This is not easy to do—it means, for one thing, that I was wrong about many things and for another, that part of my personality, part of my dreams, is gone. We will never have a large family and live in a big house in the country where I play the classic role of wife and mother. We are more likely to have four children at the most, and probably less, live in an apartment or suburban house (horrors!), always be a little behind, and I shall most likely work all the time, except for maternity leaves, not only because we will need the money but also because I really need the stimulation of a job— especially a teaching job. I made a great effort to turn myself into a wife-mother type, like the majority of other girls, because I do believe this is the best way to be, but I wasted my energy, because I can *never* be like they are. I love David and being with him, I love cooking, and although I don't like routine housework, I can do it with toleration. Yet, this is just not enough.

October 2, 1956

Paris Review returned "Morning of Illusion" yesterday, but
with an attached note saying they were interested in my work
and wanted to see more soon, which is a good deal of encouragement (especially coming after *Mademoiselle*'s similar comments) at this stage, about a story written quickly. . . . Although my mind is chock-full of ideas, and, if I work hard, I
can hit the jackpot in 1957 or 1958, right now I have not one
minute for writing, which makes me very frustrated.

August 2, 1957

For the past week Jonathan [her second child] has not slept at
all unless he was rocked to sleep and even now I am rocking
him with a foot and trying to write. I don't believe I've had
more than two hours a day to myself (from 6 A.M. to 11 P.M.),
and even those hours are divided up into fifteen-minute
periods. I am a cauldron of seething frustration, furious at having to continually rock the baby (I guess I spend 3 hours a day
doing just that) so that he won't wake David, who finally
dropped off to sleep.

September 6, 1957

Crying has become my daily companion. Jim and I have almost no time together. No Jim, no God, no writing—is this
what life is—bondage to children and them alone? For what?
Is there nothing else? God knows, I don't hate my children, I
love them, but I don't want to give up my life and everything I
am to them. I feel such a failure in every respect; it seems I can
do nothing—many, many women do more without any sort of
upset. Yet, I want to cry, I am *me,* not anyone else, and this is
not for me.

February 17, 1959

Yeats is right, but I cannot choose—I want perfection of the life and the art—and—worse yet—am willing to sacrifice nothing, absolutely nothing, to achieve it! More writing and less reading.

July 8, 1959

Amazing how all goes well when I am writing. I cease to worry about money or to want things, but rest within the delights of my work. If only I could always be like this! Not that I think the duality that troubles me will ever completely disappear—I love the boys too much and this love ties me to many conventional values for them. One can choose the unorthodox for oneself, but I don't know if it is fair to children to make such a choice for them.

November 29, 1959

Oh, how I'd like to be able to write poetry again!

October 18, 1960

Well, we finally did buy a house.

I have been reflecting, in odd moments throughout this entire house hunting enterprise on what has happened to my own thinking these past ten years so that I am overjoyed to be moving into such a house [in the Washington D.C. suburbs] and creating my ambiance there instead of in a Roman studio or London flat. Have I gone the way of everyone else, settling finally for mediocrity, conformity and the rest? (Or perhaps I have been in error about that mythical "everyone else"?) What has happened to my belief in my own uniqueness?

October 24, 1960

Joanne [Greenburg, author of *I Never Promised You a Rose Garden*] asks "are you fulfilled?"—without writing, that is. No, no—although, like her, I wish I could be, for everything would be simplified. My euphoria of the past six weeks has given way to restlessness and irritation as I fight, in vain, for a few free hours of silence for my work. The children remain marvelous, I am still committed to hearth and home—but, damn it, that is not all, not enough. I need time to discipline my spirit away from visions of material delight as I think of my new house, and time for reading, thinking and writing would relieve the necessity for making these visions carry so much of the burden of my imagination.

January 8, 1961

I simply am unable to believe in the cosmic importance of much that most other people (not Jim, bless him!) hold important, and I never have been able to change. I turned down the Sol Hurock job, I chose the New School over schools with more name, I married Jim instead of the professional man my family expected, then had a baby immediately—all decisions against a certain kind of success which makes material things, the transient, more important than anything else.

I grow upset, angry, depressed beyond all measure at the amount of time and effort we give to mutable things. Houses fall into disrepair—paint peels, walls crack, dirt accumulates —cars slowly die, clothes wear out—yet, to these we give our greatest loyalties. All the vast mechanical resources are mobilized to produce—a can opener!

It is this despair at the mutability of all created things that links the Artist and the Ascetic—a desire to purify and preserve—to set oneself apart—somehow—from the river flowing onward to the grave. The philosopher shares it, too—I have been thinking of Plato this entire time. . . .

What I hope to do is to make of art a discipline strong enough, when coupled with religion, to resist meaninglessness.

July 10, 1961

Jim and I have just stopped going to church, without talking about it as yet or facing what this means to the children and to our other commitments. The immediate reason is our decision to make sure we have no other children; of course, many Catholics use birth control and continue to attend church, even receiving the Sacraments, but this is meaningless to me. However, the reason for my decision on contraceptives is that I no longer am able to believe in any operative sense. For a time, belief changed me, and my life was a genuine commitment, but for the past year this has been less and less so. I remain locked in this selfish, middle-class world, and whatever impulses I feel to break out of it come from my writing, not religion. To believe implies, among other things, "thy will be done," and from the evidence, God's will was that I should make a holocaust of my abilities and have many children. Well, I cannot accept that, have now taken positive steps to insure this not happening, and from this refusal to accept "Thy will be done" in the Catholic framework has come everything else, my other religious failures, because I've been against all of this in my heart.

I don't know what will happen in the future—after all my twistings and turnings of the past ten years, I refuse to predict. Right now I am free floating.

March 1, 1962

I have set up my life for writing so much that when I face a few days with no daily stint, I feel dispossessed of myself. I wonder how satisfactory a mother I am and do not know. There are always those necessary hours at the typewriter . . . it is difficult to know.

February 14, 1964

Forgot how good Wright Morris's *The Territory Ahead* is—better than anything Leslie Fiedler attempts. But it set me off on my own train of thought about American fiction and myself (also, many writers in similar situations). We hear *ad nauseum* of "The American Experience." Yet, such resounding pieties are not the proper home of the writer. So, turning from that, we find that the American experience is the experience of Americans, that he is an American and it is his experience, seen without the burden of cliché but as simply, as uniquely, as possible, for me. This means that my relationship to America, on the one hand, and to the tradition of English fiction on which ours was based, on the other hand, is highly qualified. My language *is* English. But I have more in common with the psychology and milieu of Russian or French novelists, and with reason. What of America has my background given me except a myth, fleshed out by schoolroom platitudes? This myth and the consequent state of mind of someone exposed to it, is one pole which determines imaginative response, but there is another pole, on the reality of which the myth is abraded—the connection with Europe and that dark past. Descendants of immigrants desperately seek to avoid it—hence, the familiar "American" manner—but the writer cannot. The American writer owes much less to English literature than gentility (and Lionel Trilling) supposes.

For myself, this oblique vantage point is a plus, the tension fruitful. The way of so many from the slum to the common room is not the way for a novelist unless he comes by it naturally—and then he has his own problems as he wrestles with his own material.

July 20, 1964

Certain thoughts haunt me—they must somehow go into my work. First, there is this business of connections. I remember myself in the autumn of 1962 pushing Sarah [her daughter] on the swing in our yard and reading Freud's *Civilization and Its Discontents*, or, when we lived on Sargent Road walking to the bus past the scrub lots, past rows of brick houses, reading Virginia Woolf, or this past Saturday—the worst—coming home from the library with a stackful of books—poetry, photographs, after a morning of reading *The London Magazine*. The bus goes through hellish Negro slums, condemned houses, streets torn up, noise of machines, bloody heat, dust, grit, stench of sweat and alcohol, nothing that would link these people with the world of the books. Not even their vestigial Christianity. How to make art of such life.

My own days—how many writers spend hours each day washing, ironing, cleaning, making beds, etc. No serious intellectual life possible under such conditions. Under the circumstances, a diminution. How to set up artist's life against the prevailing conditions.

August 14, 1964

Too much week to write about. House sold. . . . By October we'll be out, back in the city somewhere—Southwest, Georgetown, Glover Park—wherever we can find what we want at a rent we can afford. Away from these dreadful neighbors and our sense of isolation. A sense of elation paralleling the depression I had when we bought the house. Curious.

Even more curious, but showing how deep the psychic roots—for the first time in *nine* years, I am writing poetry. Good poetry. Completely different than my earlier work and free of the flaws that clog my prose—a simple language, direct emotion, all very smooth as if—as if, I don't know, though. The novel is all choked up, going nowhere, nowhere to go right now, no stories—and then this flowering in the midst of my exhaustion.

April 27, 1965

Alternate between great confidence in my work and killing depression. Everything is new, language simpler, diction firm—so much so that I cannot even begin to revise old stories, they were written by another person altogether, but there are still old problems, digging deeper into the past—mine, my feelings dealing with the unpleasant—how slowly it all goes.

June 8, 1965

I talk too much!

I am too matronly and confined, too dull and restrained, even for an affair. With three children? Impossible. And with what man in Washington?

Hello, August Strindberg!

September 12, 1965

Almost sure that I am pregnant—either that or I am very sick indeed. . . . Just when all the children are off in school at last! How and why did it happen? And yet, I'm not unhappy, only concerned about two things—that Jim won't get his government promotion and that we will have to move next summer. . . . If this baby could be more pleasure with—for once— less worry about money—I'd be quite easy in my mind.

In any case, my doubts about my novelistic abilities grow. . . . . Less and less do the signs of current literary life touch me—but to find myself in my own poetry—that is what I would give my life for.

February 10, 1966

We move on the 15th—hooray! Another new life. But not enough. Only to try. And I must first defeat myself, this tendency to be less the artist than the middle class wifeling. Absolutely wrong for all of us! All right, kid, let's see the poetry!

June 2, 1966

The kind of life I am leading now is the submerged life, unknown as far as poetry is concerned. Ginsberg and his crew, all the fags, the drug people—ok, but that is not all there is. Another life—I know it, for it is mine.

How different a woman's perceptions would have to be, just based on her experience! How can I give adherence to an idea when I see how ideas retreat before the very small bits of reality that make up a day?

July 8, 1966

Cleaning a closet, I found a box of my old manuscripts and quotations. Threw a lot away, only glanced at the stories and novel, found some pages good, some bad, all stamped with *me* one way or another. Most curious were forgotten early poems on the same themes as the ones I am working on now—death, mutability. Notes for essays (one on Pavese, for example), and anthology lists were good—I could have made a career in literature, it is not just my remembered impressions.

But I did not want to, still do not. The same impulses run through my life now as always—I am not ambitious, for all my intelligence and drive. I want the deep hidden life. It is a strong religious impulse, for all my outward waywardness.

That is one dominant thread that appears in my work. The other is my bookishness. Words, reading and writing, will mark my life no matter what else I do. I doubt that I shall have affairs or bother my children when they are grown, for my real passion always goes to writing.

Most curious—the way I clutter up my mind with trivia, history dates, etc., but let my past, myself as I was, slip into limbo so that I am constantly being surprised by what I have read, written, what I was. Perhaps this is the lack in my work, what prevents me from leaping into the full power which is mine—that I cannot face myself, have not been able to come to recognition of my past, myself.

How to do it?

Practically all of my life is invisible.

Matthew [her fourth and last child] is a joyful baby—he looks intelligent and happy already all the time.

The life I am leading, which I could not imagine from my first 20 years, has been good because it has forced me to be quiet and to deepen. But there is one great flaw—how much energy and emotion goes to tiny, fleeting facts of daily life! How easy to sink beneath the weight of newspapers, laundry, report cards, supermarkets and all the rest.

July 20, 1966

A night of dreams, despite my exhaustion. Dreams, which refresh Jim, leave me feeling dead the next day, far away and useless. I don't remember the sequence of events, but the main figures were myself and a couple with four daughters and a baby boy. I am caring for this boy, bending over to put him in a tub or carriage, when they approach me. The wife and girls are timid, unimportant. The man is large and stocky with gray, crew-cut hair. He is a poet! And he recognizes me as a poet! Over the baby, over the heads of his daughters, over the conversation of domestic matters, he sees that I am a poet.

June 10, 1967

Fewer and fewer things interest me any more. I do not write here often, my language becomes clumsy, my poetry is never complete, I have no faith in myself. I rush past things—my children, the savor of each day, pushing ahead into the future. Why? Because I am 34 and know that life is short. I have accomplished nothing of what I wished to accomplish. And what was that? Really, I wanted the impossible. A man could do it, perhaps, but not a woman. I wanted to *become somebody,* an artist entire, beginning with nothing, nothing at all—no roots, no money, no parental help, no culture, no father—to create myself from scratch through language only, to see my face without a mirror. And I have failed, naturally. Everything else that I have—and it is a lot—has lost its savor because of that failure. Praise is empty. I have accomplished nothing of what I intended and I never shall. The children do not make up for that. They have their own destinies and I have just a succession of days.

August 26, 1967

How much of myself I have stopped writing about! Am I less present to myself or more? But the language of such knowledge withers, perhaps to mold that will enrich poetry, perhaps not. Without fiction or journal, the record passes silently.

During the day I live intensely—combing my hair, I connect the inner flashes, lying on the bed at 7:00 I watch the leaves, the sun, the shadows and . . . my day runs on, time runs out and it is gone.

Have I made the right choice? I don't know, will never know. But you can't have both. My old talking, the quick words that said immediately that I was clever—all gone. Slowness, silence in return. It is another life with children.

April 16, 1968

It is as if my whole body were flowing out in words like blood and only a husk is left for everything else.

May 6, 1968

Finished my first children's book.

July 27, 1968

Well, all my growing secret fears—of this summer, of my whole life, I suppose—are out in the open now. It is not only the operation—which will be bad enough and finish me as I was—it is that more and more I believe that the doctor will do nothing because it will be too late and I am riddled with cancer and dying, leaving all these children, especially Matthew, whose life will be broken in two forever—Sarah, too. All of this for no reason, no meaning, absolutely without purpose. At best, my life broken. At worst, my suspicions, a wretched death at 35—just like that, when my poems and translations are coming to fulfillment, when my children's book will probably be accepted—all too late. I have always been most afraid of living and dying like a grain of sand on a beach, accomplishing nothing, and so it will be. I am not surprised but stunned and terrified. I am nothing of a heroine, not brave, and I did not want this—yet why have I always supected that I would be asked to pay for all I have? At the same time, what good my gifts if they demand my life? I expect nothing more, there will be nothing more but a painful end.

August 28, 1968

I was in the hospital from July 28 to August 15. First, there was the radical mastectomy for a fast-growing and ugly cancer which may still be alive in the nodes. Then there was a complete hysterectomy to make certain the cancer had not travelled and also to eliminate the hormones which cause the rapid growth of a cancer like the one I had. That operation was awful—three days of constant pain and discomfort. And there is radiation yet to go, with no certainty that all will be well even then.

Right now I feel good and want to get back to my normal schedule. I find even quasi-invalidism discouraging. There are weekly visits to the doctor to have fluid drained from my arm and chest, there are ugly and depressing scars, there are some adjustments. There is, above all, a sense of doors closing, youth forever over, a sense of becoming a victim, one of those people who are shunned or pitied out of the crippled emotions of others. No new dimensions opening, old ones closing. I, who have always hated my body, now am justified—it has betrayed me and turned ugly and deserves to be hated.

I have rooted my poems and my thought in a complex reality, believing that the power of the world is real. And now I see that this is indeed so and the toughness of the artist is to know this, yet not to succumb. The glory of the later years lies in this knowledge. The ecstatic poetry of today or the poetry of Bly and his followers believes that verbal symbols can deny these incompatibilities. But the world *is* real and the flesh takes its revenge.

October 27, 1968

Such a long time without writing—but the daily routine does not change and there is little to say about it except that it leaves almost no time for anything but itself—reminding me quite often of Hannah Arendt's distinction between work and labor. Labor consumes itself. So it is here—even now I look at the clock, knowing that in a few minutes I must set the table and make vegetables for dinner.

Mainly I wanted to reflect on getting older, gains and only a few losses—so many things once cared about, no longer so—more detachment and withdrawal, less passion, more reserve and tranquility—becoming more myself. And that is good.

December 25, 1968

This book ends with this year, although the pages are not quite full, despite the three years it has taken me to come this far. Will I have three more years? to fill another such book? I think not.

In 1965 no Matthew, no cancer, no poems published as the year began. Now it is possible to see how my life has changed. This Christmas was good, despite my illness. Jim made a real effort to make it so.

Right now I am tired after too little sleep, too much work last week, a busy month ahead, more shots, a lot of time at the doctor's, too much to do. My life drains away, my days disappear. But many of them are good. Perhaps it will be enough. Only, I want more! My relatives are all generous—they think I will die soon—and in all likelihood I shall—and there will be nothing I can do about it. The time is pruned out away from me. And the children—they need me and they won't have me. No difference whether I can stand this knowledge or not, it will come. Meanwhile, much happiness.

And a new year. All I ask now is to live through it healthy—and the rest of us, too.

February 18, 1969

Poetry is not enough, there is also the life to be lived—but what if one uses up the energy needed for the other? A hellish circle. Yet spending yields more than saving and it is necessary to transcend oneself.

March 4, 1969

Reading—Stieglitz, Blackmur. Then the hospital and Sarah's tonsillectomy and women with bubble hairdos—from the center of one world, the other does not exist. The only bridge between them is the stretched-out body.

March 18, 1969

Continuing my typed notes of yesterday, I can see that I am not really well. A sore tongue today and I am panicked—is the lesion cancer? And I tell myself yes. Suddenly the entire balance and order of my body is upset and I feel pains everywhere.

Then, too, I see the meaning of my sudden yearning for clothes, my desire to be fashionable, my preoccupation with earrings and sunglasses, my spending so much money on myself—a way of asserting that I will be here, be around, wearing those clothes. Dear God, I don't believe it!

September 15, 1969

A year and a little more—does such a disease never end? Or does it simply become more private, more secret? One cannot talk about it forever—even catastrophe becomes boring—and daily life is mercifully prepossessing, but there is always a noontime shadow.

February 4, 1970

More poems returned—good ones this time. *Very* depressed, more than I can say. My life questioned to its roots, all my assumptions. Intolerable anxiety—until an illusion comes into view to help me continue—to what? Dear God, I am alone and in desperate trouble!

April 10, 1970

Another beautiful day—bliss! Seabury Press is going to publish *Nellie Cameron*—and the editor is coming to Washington on the 25th to confer with me about it.

June 3, 1970

Working on poetry again just like that and I know in myself the meaning of *vocation,* because that is the sense I have, of an inner directing voice assuring me that I am touching the center of *my* existence, no matter what anyone else sees or praises me for, whether children's books or reviews, or any other life—social life, school—no, nothing else touches the experience of poetry.

October 8, 1970

I remember as the most exquisitely happy moment of my life when I first sensed myself as a whole, unique individual, all me and separate in every fiber of my consciousness. I was a child then and unaware of the loneliness of this separation, but even now I cannot regret it or wish for a return to a more undifferentiated stage. Even when I am unhappy, I rejoice in feeling *fully* the sense of myself, skin, bones, and mind, all unhappy.

November 2, 1970

Went to the doctor today, and he was just delighted that I've done so well so far—not that I can count on any time at all for three more years—and even after then, I will be lucky to live, because the survival rate is not good beyond five years. 50% death rate within 15 years. Still, my posthumous life has been good so far, and I cherish all of it and pray for it to continue.

April 24, 1972

39 tomorrow and where am I? MacDowell Colony says no. One poem accepted and a dozen rejected. And what I feel is that my poems are slack, not holding together, larger and more ambitious than earlier ones, yet not so complete and in their own lives. Everything is still all bits and pieces, all future, nothing solid. Christ at the same distance. My own ego is the lion in the path. How go beyond? How? Where find my dreams? Where rescue them from where they are hiding? Not a good year, not getting better. So much work, so many years, and I am still at the border and travelling in the dark. No use even pretending that I keep a journal—reviewing consumes *that* energy, and it is not good, but I am addicted to the money and the books. It is wrong to put so much faith in *The Crystal Nights* and the unwritten Simone Weil book, when there are so many imponderables—my talent, the market, the times— maybe I do not have it. How far I am from my early dreams— remember Gide, Valéry, J. P. Jacobsen, Rilke, the orgy of reading Lawrence and Dostoevsky? Gone, gone. . . . What will this coming year bring? My prayer will be for poems, a breakthrough into authenticity—and to be able to write the

Weil book as I would like to—deep, original, solid. I don't know if I can do it. I don't know.

May 25, 1972

I think of abandoning writing—that is abandoning myself—to teach or write for money. After so much? I think it is age, the end—the lingering end—of my youthful dreams and belief in my talent and inviolability. Even after 1968 I believed all would be well, my books would be published and success come—but it gets more difficult, more complex—the books make very little money and the work is even more difficult. . . .

May 18, 1973

Good reviews of both my books.

September 17, 1973

Beginning of the final stage for me, known and predicted five years ago and now being played out—exactly how not known but the result not in doubt. How stupid it is! I had always anticipated middle age, not youth, as the best part of my life and work, and here I am 40—facing an unpretty death within five years. And it's all totally out of control—me, who likes so much to be in control! I am not especially angry or frightened—yet—only curiously calm and alienated from what is happening, fighting to separate the *me* from the body it is in.

It shouldn't be. I've had a hard life and I deserve time to see the children grow up and take their places in the world—I'd like that—as well as to have some time with Jim when we have a little money and can enjoy our time together—we never had that, since David was born 10 months after we were married. And I need time for my poetry, since I'm coming into my own very slowly. That's one thing I couldn't rush even though I could rush through school and children. There should be time for this—and there won't be and nothing will replace that.

When I think of the poetry, I get most depressed. This is what I was born to do—and now. . . .

My optimism is leaking away out of the sieve of reality.

October 22, 1973

In to work today and feeling good and then, just as I walked in the door, Jim Andrews of Sheed & Ward called to say that they were going to publish my poems! I didn't talk to him about anything else because I was so excited. So that's the tradeoff—my life for my poems. And didn't I always secretly know it all these calm and ripening years.

November 17, 1973

If I could live in reasonably good condition to finish the novel and see my book of poems in print, I'd be ready to die. Not happy. Not wanting to leave Jim and the children. Not at 41. Too young, too soon. But I don't want to linger on in pain and weakness, in and out of hospitals, unable to work, hoping and despairing and eating away at Jim's and the children's lives. Oh, for six good months, though!

November 30, 1973

All of a sudden everything has changed dramatically for the worst, and I'm at the end—three, six, nine months is the story and I wonder if I'll be alive to see my poems published, probably not if Jim Andrews doesn't send them along soon. And I've got to make arrangements for the second book of poems—retyping and editing—redo my will, try to finish *Dacia's War* somehow—but how?—and leave letters to Jim and the children. Sort out my reviews, clip them and bundle them. All the while being tired and in pain.

December 5, 1973

Nothing will be possible. It is only a matter of time. I won't see my poems published or my book finished or the second book underway. Even my handwriting is that of a dying person. All I want to do is sleep and die.

December 13, 1973

Dear God, help me to try with all that is in me to help Jim as he has helped me—no one has ever been so marvelous to another person—and I don't deserve it.

December 25, 1973

Last evening was transcendent—Bob celebrated a liturgy here for us and the Hunts, Joan and her mother, Doris Grumbach.
. . . and it was for me a true healing experience, the center of our holiday. . . . More than anything else, I'm overwhelmed by the feelings I seem to have evoked in other people—impossible to believe, stunning me. Beautiful letter from Tillie Olsen, superb gift from Bob—tremendous love, amazing grace.

January 11, 1974

I have changed, more than I can indicate, and one of the clearest indications is in my reading—I can't *bear* to read most books, my mind skims over the words without taking anything in, there's no possibility of any sympathetic current or understanding. My mind is sluggish, it wants to sink down to the depths and rest there. And then speak simply and directly, which is the hardest thing to do. I feel that my authenticity is trapped inside me by fear, habit, custom, and I will die without being able to express it in my words, my poems. What I feel is joy, vulnerability, a desire to create, a coming to God—a sense of grasping what is deeper and stiller—and a hesitation about expressing this, an unconquered shyness. A growth in silence. Hiding in my house.

February 13, 1974

Don't we poets all delude ourselves at one time or another with tales of our talent or importance? Either we wait too long for recognition and grow bitter in the waiting, or experience it too early and must live out a long decline.

March 9, 1974

And then, each time, the fear that this is the beginning of the end—one doesn't receive a formal announcement in the mail, after all, for it remains ambiguous to the end, I'm sure.

Michele Murray died on March 14, 1974.

MARGARET WALKER

On Being Female,
Black, and Free

My birth certificate reads female, Negro, date of birth and place. Call it fate or circumstance, this is my human condition. I have no wish to change it from being female, black, and free. I like being a woman. I have a proud black heritage, and I have learned from the difficult exigencies of life that freedom is a philosophical state of mind and existence. The mind is the only place where I can exist and feel free. In my mind I am absolutely free.

My entire career of writing, teaching, lecturing, yes, and raising a family is determined by these immutable facts of my human condition. As a daughter, a sister, a sweetheart, a wife, a mother, and now a grandmother, my sex or gender is preeminent, important, and almost entirely deterministic. Maybe

95

my glands have something to do with my occupation as a creative person. About this, I am none too sure, but I think the cycle of life has much to do with the creative impulse and the biorhythms of life must certainly affect everything we do.

Creativity cannot exist without the feminine principle, and I am sure God is not merely male or female but He-She—our Father-Mother God. All nature reflects this rhythmic and creative principle of feminism and femininity: the sea, the earth, the air, fire, and all life whether plant or animal. Even as they die, are born, grow, reproduce, and grow old in their cyclic time, so do we in lunar, solar, planetary cycles of meaning and change.

Ever since I was a little girl I have wanted to write and I have been writing. My father told my mother it was only a puberty urge and would not last, but he encouraged my early attempts at rhyming verses just the same, and he gave me the notebook or daybook in which to keep my poems together. When I was eighteen and had ended my junior year in college, my father laughingly agreed it was probably more than a puberty urge. I had filled the 365 pages with poems.

Writing has always been a means of expression for me and for other black Americans who are just like me, who feel, too, the need for freedom in this "home of the brave, and land of the free." From the first, writing meant learning the craft and developing the art. Going to school had one major goal, to learn to be a writer. As early as my eighth year I had the desire, at ten I was trying, at eleven and twelve I was learning, and at fourteen and fifteen I was seeing my first things printed in local school and community papers. I have a copy of a poem published in 1930 and an article with the caption, "What Is to Become of Us?" which appeared in 1931 or 1932. All of this happened before I went to Northwestern.

I spent fifteen years becoming a poet before my first book appeared in 1942. I was learning my craft, finding my voice, seeking discipline as life imposes and superimposes that discipline upon the artist. Perhaps my home environment was most important in the early stages—hearing my mother's music, my sister and brother playing the piano, reading my father's books, hearing his sermons, and trying every day to write a poem. Meanwhile, I found I would have to start all over again and learn how to write prose fiction in order to write the novel I was determined to create to the best of my ability and thus fulfill my promise to my grandmother. A novel is not written exactly the same way as a poem, especially a long novel and a short poem. The creative process may be basically the same—that is, the thinking or conceptualization—but the techniques, elements, and form or craft are decidedly and distinctively different.

It has always been my feeling that writing must come out of living, and the writer is no more than his personality endures in the crucible of his times. As a woman, I have come through the fires of hell because I am a black woman, because I am poor, because I live in America, and because I am determined to be both a creative artist and maintain my inner integrity and my instinctive need to be free.

I don't think I noticed the extreme discrimination against women while I was growing up in the South. The economic struggle to exist and the racial dilemma occupied all my thinking until I was more than an adult woman. My mother had undergone all kinds of discrimination in academia because of her sex; so have my sisters. Only after I went back to school and earned a doctorate did I begin to notice discrimination against me as a woman. It seems the higher you try to climb, the more rarefied the air, the more obstacles appear. I realize I had been naïve, that the issues had not been obvious and that as early as my first employment I felt the sting of discrimination because I am female.

I think it took the women's movement to call my attention to cases of overt discrimination that hark back to my WPA days on the Writers' Project. It did not occur to me that Richard Wright as a supervisor on the project made $125 per month and that he claimed no formal education, but that I had just graduated from Northwestern University and I was a junior writer making $85 per month. I had no ambitions to be an administrator; I was too glad to have a job; I did not think about it. Now I remember the intense antagonism on the project toward the hiring of a black woman as a supervisor, none other than the famous Katherine Dunham, the dancer, but it never occurred to me then that she was undergoing double discrimination.

When I first went to Iowa and received my master's degree that year there were at least five or six women teaching English in the university. When I returned to study for the doctorate, not a single woman was in the department. At Northwestern my only woman teacher had taught personal hygiene. I did not expect to find women at Yale, but it slowly dawned on me that black women in black colleges were more numerous than white women in coed white universities.

And then I began looking through the pages of books of American and English literature that I was teaching, trying in vain to find the works of many women writers. I have read so many of those great women writers of the world—poets, novelists, and playwrights: Sigrid Undset and Selma Lagerlof, Jane Austen, George Sand, George Eliot, and Colette. All through the ages women have been writing and publishing, black and white women in America and all over the world. A few women stand out as geniuses of their times, but those are all too few. Even the women who survive and are printed, published, taught and studied in the classroom fall victim to negative male literary criticism. Black women suffer damages at the hands of every male literary critic, whether he is black or white. Occasionally a man grudgingly admits that some woman writes well, but only rarely.

Despite severe illness and painful poverty, and despite jobs that always discriminated against me as a woman—never paying me equal money for equal work, always threatening or replacing me with a man or men who were neither as well educated nor experienced but just men—despite all these examples of discrimination I have managed to work toward being a self-fulfilling, re-creating, reproducing woman, raising a family, writing poetry, cooking food, doing all the creative things I know how to do and enjoy. But my problems have not been simple; they have been manifold. Being female, black, and poor in America means I was born with three strikes against me. I am considered at the bottom of the social class-caste system in these United States, born low on the totem pole. If "a black man has no rights that a white man is bound to respect," what about a black woman?

Racism is so extreme and so pervasive in our American society that no black individual lives in an atmosphere of freedom. The world of physical phenomena is dominated by fear and greed. It consists of pitting the vicious and the avaricious against the naïve, the hunted, the innocent, and the victimized. Power belongs to the strong, and the strong are BIG in more ways than one. No one is more victimized in this white male American society than the black female.

There are additional barriers for the black woman in publishing, in literary criticism, and in promotion of her literary wares. It is an insidious fact of racism that the most highly intellectualized, sensitized white person is not always perceptive about the average black mind and feeling, much less the creativity of any black genius. Racism forces white humanity to underestimate the intelligence, emotion, and creativity of black humanity. Very few white Americans are conscious of the myth about race that includes the racial stigmas of inferiority and superiority. They do not understand its true economic and political meaning and therefore fail to understand its social purpose. A black, female person's life as a writer is fraught with conflict, competitive drives, professional rivalries, even danger, and deep frustrations. Only when she escapes to a spiritual world can she find peace, quiet, and hope of freedom. To choose the life of a writer, a black female must arm herself with a fool's courage, foolhardiness, and serious purpose and dedication to the art of writing, strength of will and integrity, because the odds are always against her. The cards are stacked. Once the die is cast, however, there is no turning back.

In the first place, the world of imagination in which the writer must live is constantly being invaded by the enemy, the mundane world. Even as the worker in the fires of imagination finds that the world around her is inimical to intellectual activity, to the creative impulse, and to the kind of world in which she must daily exist and also thrive and produce, so, too, she discovers that she must meet that mundane world head-on every day on its own terms. She must either conquer or be conquered.

A writer needs certain conditions in which to work and create art. She needs a piece of time; a peace of mind; a quiet place; and a private life.

Early in my life I discovered I had to earn my living and I would not be able to eke out the barest existence as a writer.

Nobody writes while hungry, sick, tired, and worried. Maybe you can manage with one of these but not all four at one time. Keeping the wolf from the door has been my full-time job for more than forty years. Thirty-six of those years I have spent in the college classroom, and nobody writes to full capacity on a full-time teaching job. My life has been public, active, and busy to the point of constant turmoil, tumult, and trauma. Sometimes the only quiet and private place where I could write a sonnet was in the bathroom, because that was the only room where the door could be locked and no one would intrude. I have written mostly at night in my adult life and especially since I have been married, because I was determined not to neglect any members of my family; so I cooked every meal daily, washed dishes and dirty clothes, and nursed sick babies.

I have struggled against dirt and disease as much as I have against sin, which, with my Protestant and Calvinistic background, was always to be abhorred. Every day I have lived, however, I have discovered that the value system with which I was raised is of no value in the society in which I must live. This clash of my ideal with the real, of my dream world with the practical, and the mystical inner life with the sordid and ugly world outside—this clash keeps me on a battlefield, at war, and struggling, even tilting windmills. Always I am determined to overcome adversity, determined to win, determined to be me, myself at my best, always female, always black, and everlastingly free. I think this is always what the woman writer wants to be, herself, inviolate, and whole. Shirley Chisholm, who is also black and female, says she is unbossed and unbought. So am I, and I intend to remain that way. Nobody can tell me what to write because nobody owns me and nobody pulls my strings. I have not been writing to make money or earn my living. I have taught school as my vocation. Writing is my life, but it is an avocation nobody can buy. In this respect I believe I am a free agent, stupid perhaps, but *me* and still free.

When I was younger I considered myself an emancipated woman, freed from the shackles of mind and body that typified the Victorian woman, but never would I call myself the liberated woman in today's vernacular; never the bohemian; never the completely free spirit living in free love; never the lesbian sister; always believing in moderation and nothing to excess; never defying convention, never radical enough to defy tradition; not wanting to be called conservative but never moving beyond the bounds of what I consider the greatest liberty within law, the greatest means of freedom within control. I have lived out my female destiny within the bonds of married love. For me, it could not have been otherwise. In the same way I refuse to judge others, for if tolerance is worth anything, love is worth everything. Everyone should dare to love.

I am therefore fundamentally and contradictorily three things. I am religious almost to the point of orthodoxy—I go to church, I pray, I believe in the stern dogma and duty of Protestant Christianity; I am radical but I wish to see neither the extreme radical left nor the radical right in control. And I am like the astrological description of a crab, a cancer—quick to retreat into my shell when hurt or attacked. I will wobble around circuitously to find another way out when the way I have chosen has been closed to me. I believe absolutely in the power of my black mind to create, to write, to speak, to witness truth, and to be heard.

Enough for a time about being female and black. What about freedom? The question of freedom is an essential subject for any writer. Without freedom, personal and social, to write as one pleases and to express the will of the people, the writer is in bondage. This bondage may seem to be to others outside oneself but closely related by blood or kinship in some human fashion; or this bondage may appear to be to the inimical forces of the society that so impress or repress that individual.

For the past twenty years or longer I have constantly come into contact with women writers of many different races, classes, nationalities, and degrees. I look back on more than forty years of such associations. Whether at a cocktail party for Muriel Rukeyser at *Poetry* magazine or at Yaddo where Carson MacCullers, Jean Stafford, Karen Blixen, Caroline Slade, and Katherine Anne Porter were guests; or meeting Adrienne Rich and Erica Jong in Massachusetts at Amherst, or having some twenty-five of my black sister-poets at a Phillis Wheatley poetry festival here in Mississippi, including many of the young and brilliant geniuses of this generation; or here in Mississippi where I have come to know Eudora Welty and Ellen Douglas, or having women from foreign countries journey to Jackson to see me, women like Rosey Pool from Amsterdam and a young woman writer a few weeks ago from Turkey or Bessie Head from South Africa—all these experiences have made me know and understand the problems of women writers and our search for freedom.

For the nonwhite woman writer, whether in Africa, Asia, Latin America, the islands of the Caribbean, or the United States, her destiny as a writer has always seemed bleak. Women in Africa and Asia speak of hunger and famine and lack of clean water at the same time that their countries are riddled with warfare. Arab women and Jewish women think of their children in a world that has no hope of peace. Irish women, Protestant and Catholic, speak of the constant threat of bombs and being blown to bits. The women of southern Africa talk of their lives apart from their husbands and their lives in exile from their homelands because of the racial strife in their countries. A Turkish woman speaks of the daily terrorism in her country, of combing the news each evening to see if there are names known on the list of the murdered.

I have read the works of scores of these women. I saw Zora Neale Hurston when I was a child and I know what a hard life she had. I read the works of a dozen black women in the Harlem Renaissance, who despite their genius received only a small success. Langston Hughes translated Gabriela Mistral, and I read her before she won the Nobel Prize for Literature. Hualing Nieh Engle tells of her native China, and my friends in Mexico speak of the unbelievable poverty of their people. Each of these internationally known women writers is my sister in search of an island of freedom. Each is part of me and I am part of her.

Writing is a singularly individual matter. At least it has historically been so. Only the creative, original individual working alone has been considered the artist working with the fire of imagination. Today, this appears no longer to be the case. In America, our affluent, electronic, and materalistic society does not respect the imaginative writer regardless of sex, race, color, or creed. It never thought highly of the female worker, whether an Emily Dickinson or Amy Lowell, Phillis Wheatley, or Ellen Glasgow. Our American society has no respect for the literary values of intellectual honesty nor for originality and creativity in the sensitive individual. Books today are managed, being written by a committee and promoted by the conglomerate, corporate structures. Best sellers are designed as commodities to sell in the marketplace before a single word is written. Plastic people who are phony writers pretending to take us into a more humanistic century are quickly designated the paper heroes who are promoted with super-HYPE. Do I sound bitter? A Black Woman Writer who is free? Free to do what? To publish? To be promoted? Of what value is freedom in a money-mad society? What does freedom mean to the racially biased and those bigots who have deep religious prejudices? What is my hope as a woman writer?

I am a black woman living in a male-oriented and male-dominated white world. Moreover, I live in an American Empire where the financial tentacles of the American Octopus in the business-banking world extend around the globe, with the multinationals and international conglomerates encircling everybody and impinging on the lives of every single soul. What then are my problems? They are the pressures of a sexist, racist, violent, and most materalistic society. In such a society life is cheap and expendable; honor is a rag to be scorned; and justice is violated. Vice and money control business, the judicial system, government, sports, entertainment, publishing, education, and the church. Every other arm of this hydra-headed monster must render lip service and yeoman support to extend, uphold, and perpetuate the syndicated world-system. The entire world of the press, whether broadcast or print journalism, must acquiesce and render service or be eliminated. And what have I to do with this? How do I operate? How long can I live under fear before I too am blown to bits and must crumble into anonymous dust and nonentity?

Now I am sixty-three. I wish I could live the years all over. I am sure I would make the same mistakes and do all the things again exactly the same way. But perhaps I might succeed a little more; and wistfully I hope, too, I might have written more books.

What are the critical decisions I must make as a woman, as a writer? They are questions of compromise, and of guilt. They are the answers to the meaning and purpose of all life; questions of the value of life lived half in fear and half in faith, cringing under the whip of tyranny or dying, too, for what one dares to believe and dying with dignity and without fear. I must believe there is more wisdom in a righteous path that leads to death than an ignominious path of living shame; that the writer is still in the avant-garde for Truth and Justice, for Freedom, Peace, and Human Dignity. I must believe that women are still in that humanistic tradition and I must cast my lot with them.

Across the world humanity seems in ferment, in war, fighting over land and the control of people's lives; people who are hungry, sick, and suffering, most of all fearful. The traditional and historic role of womankind is ever the role of the healing and annealing hand, whether the outworn modes of nurse, and mother, cook, and sweetheart. As a writer these are still her concerns. These are still the stuff about which she writes, the human condition, the human potential, the human destiny. Her place, let us be reminded, is anywhere she chooses to be, doing what she has to do, creating, healing, and always being herself. Female, Black, and Free, this is what I always want to be.

SUSAN GRIFFIN

Thoughts on Writing:
A Diary

August 7, 1979

Last night I dreamed that I wrote the beginning of this diary
in Sanskrit. The night before in a lecture (not in a dream)
Sanskrit was explained to me as "the mother of all language."
And perhaps poetry is also the mother of language. And
thought. And once again, I have solved a problem in writing
by falling asleep and dreaming. So here I pose another principle which after all is not irrelevant. Above all the act of writing calls on faith.

Here, a voice in my head, with whom I am always having
a dialogue, asks, "Faith in what?"

But I tell the voice, "Wait, that will come. Stay with the
experience because this experience renders a precise meaning."

For instance, when I was writing *Woman and Nature: The Roaring inside Her,* which is a kind of extended, long prose poem, after several months of writing little paragraphs and doing research and making plans I came across what I thought was a terrible problem. There were sides to reality that this voice could not utter. Now the idea of creating another voice, of an entirely different tone, seems obvious. But it was not then, although even then there were two other voices in me. One was the voice of despair, which said, "This will not work." And another, that calm writer of poetry, said simply, "Wait."

A few nights later I dreamt the solution: I woke with a clear idea that I needed two voices posing conflicted visions of reality.

Now in fact (and this, in retrospect, is what I find most interesting about writing that book, which took me five years), the voice of despair and the calm voice of poetry correspond exactly to those two different world views which, roughly speaking, in my book I designated as the voice of patriarchy and the voice of woman and nature, and which came to me first in a dream.

Woman and Nature: In the chapter called "Terror" a man tells a woman of the meaninglessness of the heavens. He speaks of the void. He quantifies the vastness and the void. He tells her the human body would perish in that space, and that, in that magnitude, all human meaning becomes insignificant. "He tells her how perishable she is and how little there is to perish." The voice of woman and nature answers in that chapter that the stars "are unmerciful witnesses" to his delusions, and later sings, ". . . we know these meanings reach you . . . the stars and their light we hold in our hands. . . ." Because this voice does not despair. And does not despair because it sees the physical universe as embodying meaning.

When I wrote this chapter I had in mind a poem whose first lines ("You if you were sensible/When I tell you the stars flash signals, each one dreadful,") have admonished me for years. The poem is "Under the Oak" by D. H. Lawrence. In the poem, a man speaks in an intense and anguished voice to a woman whose silliness is implied when the speaker must ask her to refrain from turning and saying to him, "The night is wonderful," after he has described his terror of the stars to her.

In the last verse of this poem Lawrence creates out of this same woman an inhuman being ("What thing better are you, what worse?"), and, linking her to the dreadful signals of the stars, he asks what she has to do with "the mysteries" of this earth, or with his "ancient curse." Finally, in words that reverberate to woman, the stars, and what we know as chance, Lawrence asks, "What place have you in my histories?"

Lawrence's words are much more complex than my voice of the patriarch in *Woman and Nature*. Still, what the stars give him is dread, and as a being in the universe he feels cursed. The woman with whom he speaks is variously insensitive and foolish ("twittering to and fro/Benath the oak . . .") or part of the mystery that has cursed him. As all these, she is either better than him or worse, but not kindred.

This emotional tone, a kind of ambivalent bitterness toward the universe and woman, informs much of modern poetry, such that there is a range from the anguished and ambivalent despair of Lawrence to the almost scientific usage of words, as sound units without sense, that is called concrete poetry. It is more or less the official artistic dogma of our age against which feminism, as an influence on poetry, is in rebellion.

But this split view of the universe and of woman is not new. Someone/thing better or worse than myself. Nature as divine or devilish. The muse, who is feminine, as cruel or benevolent.

And now the words "mother tongue," language, widen out for me, as I see that our relationship to the one who has given us birth, and to that universe which engendered our being, might be the same as our relationship to language: we must trust words and the coming of words.

And how the conflict between these two attitudes (or voices)—that of despair toward language, the muse and the universe; and that of love of language, of faith in the universe to render meaning—how this has raged in myself. And how it is played out daily in my work.

The voice of despair arrives as a kind of terror (just as I called it in *Woman and Nature*). I am certain before I begin writing a piece that I will not be able to put sentences together, or worse, that all I have to say has been said before, that there is no purpose, that there is no intrinsic authority to my own words. And that is where the struggle begins. Because I must then find the place in myself where my words have authority, some true and untouched place that does not mutter what has been said before, that speaks feelingly, enough to electrify the rhythms of speech, and make in the very telling a proof of authenticity.

This process can take days, and during those days one looks as though one is doing nothing. Here is where despair enters.

I, for instance, clean off my desk. I make telephone calls. I know I am avoiding the typewriter. I know that in my mind, where there might be words, there is simply a blankness. I may try to write and then my words bore me. At such times the whole world of words seems to be irrelevant, as if my faith in language itself had gone. And my faith cannot be restored by any sort of reasoning or logic. Now, I am in another world and I am deaf to singing.

August 9, 1979

I come back to this problem of despair in writing, myself caught up in it today, feeling a dullness about all language. In the morning I am irritable. I feel as if my sleep had been disturbed, as if a dream were intruded upon, and I am not quite certain how to proceed. This is a profound disorientation. When I am not giving forth words, I am not certain any longer who I am. But it is not like the adolescent searching for an identity; no, this state of mind has an entirely different quality, because in it there is a feeling of loss, as if my old identity, which had worked so well, which seemed to be the whole structure of the universe, were now slipping away, and all my attempts to retrieve it seem graceless, or angry, or blaming. And the old voice of protection and order in me whispers like an Iago that I betray myself.

And now I remember the substance of a revelation about faith I had a few months ago. I was walking in the woods and became aware suddenly of a knowledge that enters me in that kind of silence, especially in the presence of an organic life that is not controlled by man. This is a knowledge of a deeply peaceful kinship with all that is alive, a state of mind that language struggles to render, and yet that, paradoxically, makes me want to sing. And at the same time I became aware that the whole impulse to science in western civilization must have been born of doubt. Indeed, all the great questions of science (what is the nature of matter, what is the origin of life, what is the cause of all motion in the universe, what is light) all these began as religious questions, and remained essentially religious until the nineteenth century. So one doubts the feeling of presence, the feeling of unity with all beings, in oneself; one seeks instead a proof, "scientific," quantifiable. Sense data. So perhaps this accounts for the poetic quality of many scientific truths, and yet, also, the fact that the scientific method abolishes intuition (although indeed intuition has solved many "scientific" problems).

In *Woman and Nature* I made the voice of science, hostile to intuition, the voice of patriarchy, and all the time I wrote that book, the patriarchal voice was in me, whispering to me (the way the voice of order whispers to me now), that I had no proof for any of my writing, that I was wildly in error, that the vision I had of the whole work was absurd.

And what is this state of mind that the voice of order brings about in myself, and that is akin to scientific doubt, and to patriarchal disapproval? I want to draw a portrait of this creature of despair who inhabits me, capture her, name her. Write a phenomenology of her.

She is, for one thing, concerned with the question of efficiency. She would not have me "waste" any time. And so, to that end, she would have me know what I am going to write during any day''s work before I write it.

And now seeing these words here, I see again how similar this creature is in every way to the patriarchal voice of science, which defends its very existence with arguments of efficiency, saving labor, use, production. But underneath this rational, is fear of the loss of control, and fear of death.

Because each time I write, each time the authentic words break through, I am changed. The older order that I was collapses and dies. I lose control. I do not know exactly what words will appear on the page. I follow language. I follow the sound of the words, and I am surprised and transformed by what I record.

And so perhaps despair hides a refusal and perhaps in this refusal is that terror born of faithlessness, which keeps a guard over my thoughts, will not let dreams reach the surface of my mind.

When I had written the first draft of *Woman and Nature* the book had a disorganized quality. I had several small chapters, some a paragraph, some a few pages, and no final sequence for them. And so I put the little pieces all in a logical order, by topic, or chronology or whatever seemed most reasonable. But this order did not "work." It was like a well-built bench that had no grace, and so one did not want to sit on it.

So I began again putting the pieces together, but this time I simply followed the words intuitively, putting pieces next to one another where the transition seemed wonderful, and that was when the shape of the book began to seem beautiful to me.

I read this in a book on Jewish mysticism: "Language in its purest form, Hebrew, according to the Kabbalists, reflects the fundamental spiritual nature of the world."

Before I wrote *Woman and Nature* I knew I wanted a kind of symmetry and a kind of repetition built into the structure. At first I began to create these purposefully. But very soon they began to occur in the work quite unbidden. So, as more and more in the work I began to oppose science with a mystical view of the universe, my work took on a life of its own, and began to resemble the patterns of the universe that it envisioned.

Thoughts on Writing: A Diary   113

There is a meditation that is also an old Shamanistic practice in which one concentrates on the body of an animal, or a shell, or a tree, or a mountain, until one becomes that mountain. (This going into and becoming the other is the way of knowledge directly opposite to scientific objectification). And when one writes *about* a phenomenon, one's words begin to mimic that phenomenon, to become that which they describe.

I remember here the Buddhist formulation: you are what you see.

The phenomenology of despair. She tells me words cannot change the world. She says there is not enough time. She wants to know a purpose for every act. She is impressed only by the quantifiable material phenomenon. She is like a scale. Or a weighing machine. How many pages have been written? She is a judge without vision. She cannot play. She above all cannot *be.* She shares with the voice of patriarchy in *Woman and Nature* this idea that forests ought to grow near sawmills, that trees are good for lumber. As I write about her, large spaces of white ought to appear on the page indicating silence.

So much is sacrificed, in this civilization in which I write, to the engine God of despair. But still, the other voice, the intuitive, returns, like grass forcing its way through concrete.

> So much gladness, mother
> I am afraid I will break, oh,
> why was it
> You never spoke to me of this?

This poem that entered my mind a few nights ago and until now I have not written down and suddenly, for no reason I can see, wants to be written on this page here.

Too much an imitation of Sappho, the voice of despair says. Because she is also wholly absorbed with ideas of authorship, and who said what, and one's reputation, and respectability. She is prideful and out of her mouth speaks a whole chorus of social disapproval which ranges all the way from professors, and male doctors of law, and male authorities with awards on their breasts, such as those Virginia Woolf envisioned, to feminists, different factions of the movement, to a friend I know who disapproves of a word I find I want to use.

Too much an imitation of Sappho, she says, and no one, she says, will understand what you are saying. And this, she says, has been said over and over again. What you wanted to say is inexpressible.

That moment (last week), watching the film, when I knew the filmmaker had captured a certain shape to life, which I had seen too, felt, and then tears in my eyes, crying both for the heroine in the film and that my soul was touched this way, by this film, and that also, this feeling, which perhaps has become too rare, is, nevertheless, not unique, but old, very, very old. And no, there is no logical train of words, no scientific proof, formulating what this film is saying. No, instead, the faltering words of a young boy, which on repetition seem almost sentimental—"We cannot live without love"—these evoke in us this deep, old, old knowledge which we know, suddenly, must belong to every creature.

August 11, 1979

Now I begin the day wondering if the voice of the "other" in society (the lesbian, the Black, the Jew) takes on, both in herself and as a characteristic projected by the dominant ones, the meaning of the voice of poetry (or woman, or nature, or wildness, or darkness). Thus it is we in the class of the rejected who, it is argued, must be controlled. We *are* the problem, the scapegoat for all impulses that might change the accepted order.

The voice of despair, similarly, sees the voice of poetry (joy, playfulness, rebellious vision) as the problem. I encounter this particular kind of drama almost every day I write. I may hour after hour put off going into my study, or perhaps only for a few minutes, but the dialogue is the same. The voice of protection and order shouts at me "necessity," as if I must go to my desk and record reason's preordained words. But if I can listen past this voice, inside is another voice—accused of laziness and childishness and too many emotions—who wants to speak, who is overflowing with language, and whose words, in some unpredictable ways, always afterward, *after* they have been spoken, seem necessary to reason.

(Similarly, if women, blacks, lesbians, Jews were given "what they want," enormous social problems might be solved.)

This correlation might explain why the most interesting creative work is being done at the moment by those who are excluded and have departed from the dominant culture— women, people of color, homosexuals. And this work, unlike the decadent, and abstract, and dadaist, and concrete, and mechanist work of the dominant culture, is not despairing. This work is radiant with will, with the desire to speak; it sings with the clear tones of long-suppressed utterance, is brilliant with light, with powerful and graceful forms, with forms that embody feeling and enlarge the capacity of the beholder, of the listener, to feel.

I find myself staying away, on the whole, unless they have been recommended to me as an exception, from work by white men, because this work seems to need to blunt or even bludgeon the sensibilities of its audience. This is also true of work by women or blacks who imitate that white male contemporary tradition. And there are of course abundant examples of art by white men that depart from this tradition.

This voice of departure from protection and order is what I value most in myself. She is the one who loves, and loves fiercely (and perhaps that is why so much of poetry is love poetry). She has a sense of the largest meanings of life and can find these in the smallest actualities. If there is a tragedy, a weeping in her, this is always a grief for the loss of herself, her burial, her muteness.

Silences. Not the silences between notes of music, or the silences of a sleeping animal, or the calm of a glassy surfaced river witnessing the outstretched wings of a heron. Not the silence of an emptied mind. But this other silence. That silence which can feel like a scream, in which there is no peace. The grim silence between two lovers who are quarreling. The painful silence of the one with tears in her eyes who will not cry. The silence of the child who knows she will not be heard. The silence of a whole people who have been massacred. Of a whole sex made mute, or not educated to speech. The silence of a mind afraid to admit truth to itself. This is the silence the poet dreads.

And now I think of the wonderful laughter of a room full of women, the excited talking. The joy. Or the almost blistering crackle of energy in a room full of women when one is singing or reading her work to the others. Every word counts.

Think of the difference between these two phrases, that "things count" or to "count things."

And what of rigor, or discipline, or training? Do these belong to the voice of protection or to the voice of departure? To both now, I think, sitting here, having forced myself to come to my study before going out on errands. Because I know I will have more energy now. But perhaps the key to the difference here is intent. I speak now of the kind of joyful rigor—and now perhaps is the time to make a distinction between pleasure and joy. When one is working very hard, it may at any moment be more pleasurable to go from the work and sleep, or eat or lie in the sun. But joy, which is a different, deeper, more thrilling kind of pleasure, joy which is an experience of embodied meaning, joy may be had from working on. Even when the body complains, or the mind aches and claims it cannot go on. To find joy, even in the erotic, one must push past resistances, both in the psyche and the physical, and above all this is significant to the process of writing. But one does not intend to push past a resistance to punish oneself. Rather, one has a hunger for this joy, for this meaning that will pierce experience, and make one suddenly close to all being.

So in writing *Woman and Nature* I moved toward joy but often with great weariness and full of fear and even sometimes anguish. Because indeed the voice of protection and order *is* a resistance, and it takes great strength (courage, rigor, discipline, decisiveness) to struggle with this voice. But finally the joy was in the writing itself, to witness and be part of this process whereby the words and shape of the book began to embody its meaning, so that the very process of writing seemed a proof and to illuminate existence.

And finally I was changed by the writing of the book.

Synchronisities, the voices of trees, rivers, the wind, coincidental openings of books, a larger knowledge that seemed available to me only through "intuition" (a mode of listening to the universe) all these in my writing of the book changed me so that in my acts, in my daily acts, I was no longer a child of the age of science and rational thought. Now, writing this diary even, I still live in a profound state of disorientation. I know I find my power only when I trust language and follow words, moving with them musically, but I cannot always do this. I find myself stopping. Looking about to see where I am. Who I am. And what I am doing.

Faith in what? Only in what I know most certainly and in what can never be proved except through joy. But in this sense a diary about writing is not about writing at all. Or at least, not uniquely about writing. And if this were not so, poets would have no readers.

So all that I ask of my writing I ask of the rest of my life too. *Here (I say) the words are too thin. I have heard this before, I say, and there is more to this than is being revealed. I have said the obvious and expected. But beyond this must be something shocking, something satisfying.* And so I mark out these old words and write again. I cross out all the words except those that affect me deeply, those for which I have some "irrational" love. I keep those and build again. And again. All the while knowing that deeper meaning will rise to the surface like the form in a piece of stone, or the grain of a polished wood, if I have faith in this knowledge inside me. If I keep working. And over and over the words do not fail me. Over and over I come to a clarifying end. A circle is made. A pattern of sense is given to those words I loved for no apparent reason. I trust my own heart again. *This experience renders a precise meaning.*

ALICE WALKER

One Child of One's Own:
A Meaningful Digression
within the Work(s)

Someone asked me once whether I thought women artists
should have children, and, since we were beyond discussing
why this question is never asked artists who are men, I gave
my answer promptly.

"Yes," I said, somewhat to my surprise. And, as if to
amend my rashness, I added: "They should have children—*as-
suming this is of interest to them*—but only one."

"Why only one?" this Someone wanted to know.

"Because with one you can move," I said. "With more
than one you're a sitting duck."

In the work of this essay, and beyond this essay, I am indebted to the
courageous and generous spirits of Tillie Olsen, Barbara Smith, and Gloria
Steinem.—A.W.

121

The year after my only child, R, was born, my mother offered me uncharacteristically bad advice: "You should have another one soon," said she, "so that R will have someone to play with, and so you can get it all over with faster."

Such advice does not come from what a woman recalls of her own experience. It comes from a pool of such misguidance women have collected over the millenia to help themselves feel less foolish for having more than one child. This pool is called, desperately, pitiably, "Women's Wisdom." In fact it should be called "Women's Folly."

The rebellious, generally pithy advice that comes from a woman's own experience more often resembles my mother's automatic response to any woman she meets who pines for children but has been serenely blessed with none: "If the Lord sets you free, be free indeed." *This crafty justification of both nonconformity and a shameless reveling in the resultant freedom is what women and slaves everywhere and in every age since the Old Testament have appropriated from the Bible.*

"No, thank you," I replied. "I will never have another child out of this body again."

"But why do you say that?" she asked breathlessly, perhaps stunned by my redundancy. "You married a man who's a wonderful fatherly type. He has so much love in him he should have fifty children running around his feet."

I saw myself stamping them out from around his feet like so many ants. If they're running around his feet for the two hours between the time he comes home from the office and the time we put them to bed, I thought, they'd be underneath my desk all day. Stamp, Stamp.

My mother continued: "Why," she said, "until my fifth child I was like a young girl. I could pick up and go anywhere I wanted to." She *was* a young girl. She was still under twenty-five when her fifth child was born, my age when I became pregnant with R. Besides, since I am the last child in a family of eight, this image of nimble flight is not the one lodged forever in my mind. I remember a woman struggling to get everyone else dressed for church on Sunday and only with the greatest effort being able to get ready on time herself. But, since I am not easily seduced by the charms of painful past experience, recalled in present tranquility, I did not bring this up.

At the time my mother could "pick up and go" with five children, she and my father traveled, usually, by wagon. I can see how that would have been pleasant: it is pleasant still in some countries—in parts of China, Cuba, Jamaica, Mexico, Greece, etc., etc. A couple of slow mules, ambling along a bright southern road, the smell of pine and honeysuckle, absence of smog, birds chirping. Those five dear little voices piping up in back of the wagon seat, healthy from natural foods: Plums! Bird! Tree! Flowers! Scuppernongs! Enchanting.

"The other reason I will never have another child out of this body is because having a child *hurts*, even more than toothache (and I am sure no one who has had toothache but not childbirth can imagine this), and it changes the body."

Well, there are several responses from the general supply of Women's Folly my mother could have chosen to answer this. She chose them all.

"*That* little pain," she scoffed. (*Although, from her own experience, which, caught in a moment of weakness for truth she has let slip, she has revealed that during my very own birth the pain was so severe she could not speak, not even to tell the midwife I had been born, and that because of the pain she was sure she would die—a thought that no doubt, under the circumstances, afforded relief. Instead, she blacked out, causing me to be almost smothered by the bedclothes.*) "That pain is over before you know it." That is response #1. #2 is, "The thing about that *kind* of pain is that it does a funny thing to a woman (*Uh-oh, I thought, this is going to be the*

Women's Folly companion to the 'women sure are funny creatures,' *stuff*); looks like the more it hurts you to give birth, the more you love the child." (*Is that why she loves me so much, I wonder. Naturally, I had wanted to be loved for myself, not for her pain.*) #3. "Sometimes the pain, *they say,* isn't even real. Well, not as real as it feels at the time." (*This one deserves comment made only with blows, and is one of the reasons women sometimes experience muscle spasms around their mothers.*) And then, #4, the one that angers me most of all: "Another thing about the pain, *you soon forget it.*"

Am I mistaken in thinking I have never forgotten a pain in my life? Even those at parties, I remember.

"I remember every moment of it perfectly," I said. "Furthermore, I don't like stretch marks. I hate them, especially on my thighs" (which are otherwise gorgeous, and of which I am vain). Nobody had told me that my body, after bearing a child, would not be the same. I had heard things like: "Oh, your figure, and especially your breasts [of which I am also vain] will be better than ever." They sagged.

Well, why did I have a child in the first place?

Curiosity. Boredom. Avoiding the draft. Of these three reasons, I am redeemed only by the first. Curiosity is my natural state and has led me headlong into every worthwhile experience (never mind the others) I have ever had. It justifies itself. Boredom, in my case, means a lull in my writing, emotional distance from whatever political movement I am involved in, inability to garden, read, or daydream—easily borne if there are at least a dozen good movies around to attract me. Alas, in Jackson, Mississippi, where my husband, M, and I were living in 1968, there were few. About the draft we had three choices: the first, C.O. status for M, was immediately denied us, as was "alternative service to one's country," which meant, in his case, legally desegregating a violent, frightening, rigidly segregated Mississippi; the second was to move to Canada, which did not thrill me, but which I would gladly have done rather than have M go to prison. (Vietnam was never one of our choices.) The third was, if M could not become twenty-six years old in time, to make of him "a family man."

My bad days were spent in depression, anxiety, rage against the war and a state of apprehension over the amount of rainfall there is annually in Vancouver, and the slow rate of racial "progress" in Mississippi. (Politicians were considered "progressive" if they announced they were running for a certain office as candidates "for *all* the people;" this was a subtle—they thought—announcement to blacks that their existence was acknowledged.) I was also trying to become pregnant.

My good days were spent teaching, writing a simple history pamphlet for use in black day-care centers in Jackson, recording black women's autobiographies, making a quilt (African fabrics, Mississippi string pattern), completing my second book, a novel, and trying to become pregnant.

Three days after I finished the novel, R was born. The pregnancy: the first three months I vomited. The middle three I felt fine and flew off to look at ruins in Mexico. The last three I was so huge—I looked like someone else, which did not please me.

What is true about giving birth is . . . that it is miraculous. It might even be the one genuine miracle in life (which is, by the way, the basic belief of many "primitive" religions). The "miracle" of nonbeing, death, certainly pales, I would think, beside it. So to speak.

For one thing, though my stomach was huge and the baby

(?!) constantly causing turbulence within it, I did not believe a baby, a person, would come out of me. I mean, look what had gone *in*. (Men have every right to be envious of the womb. I'm envious of it myself, and I have one.) But there she was, coming out, a black, curling lock of hair the first part to be seen, followed by nearly ten pounds of—a human being!

Reader, I *stared*.

But this hymn of praise I, anyhow, have heard before, and will not permit myself to repeat it, since there are, in fact, very few variations, and these have become boring and shopworn. They were boring and shopworn even at the birth of Christ, which is no doubt why "Virgin Birth" and "Immaculate Conception" were all the rage.

The point is, I was changed forever. From a woman whose "womb" had been, in a sense, her head; that is to say, certain small seeds had gone in, rather different if not larger or better "creations" had come out, to a woman who had "conceived" books in her head, and had also engendered at least one human being in her body.

Well, I wondered, with great fear, where is the split in me now? What is the damage? Was it true, as "anonymous" —so often a ⸱ woman with distressing observations—warned: "Women have not created as fully as men because once she has a child a woman can not give herself to her work the way a man can . . . etc, etc?" Was I, as a writer, *done for?* So much of Women's Folly, literary and otherwise, makes us feel constricted by experience rather than enlarged by it. Curled around my baby, feeling more anger and protectiveness than love, I thought of at least two sources of folly resistance Women's Folly lacks. It lacks all conviction that women have the ability to plan their lives for periods longer than nine months, and it lacks the courage to believe that experience, and the expression of that experience, may simply be different, *unique,* rather than "greater" or "lesser." The art or literature that saves our lives *is great to us*, in any case; more than that, as a Grace Paley character might say, we do not need to know.

I was, suddenly a mother. Combating the Women's Folly in my own head was the first thing. The urge was primal: the desire to live and to appreciate my own unique life, as no one other than—myself.

It helped tremendously that by the time R was born I had no doubts about being a writer (doubts about making a *living* by writing, always). Write I did, night and day, *something,* and it was not even a choice, as having a baby was a choice, but a necessity. When I didn't write I thought of making bombs and throwing them. Of shooting racists. Of doing away—as painlessly and neatly as possible (except when I indulged in kamikaze tactics of rebellion in my daydreams) with myself. Writing saved me from the sin and *inconvenience* of violence— as it saves most writers who live in "interesting" oppressive times and are not afflicted by personal immunity.

I began to see, during a period when R and I were both ill—we had moved to Cambridge for a year and a half because I needed a change from Mississippi—that her birth, and the difficulties it provided us, joined me to a body of experience and a depth of commitment to my own life, hard to comprehend, otherwise. Her birth was the incomparable gift of seeing the world at quite a different angle than before, and judging it by standards that would apply far beyond my natural life. It also forced me to understand, viscerally, women's need for a store of Women's Folly and yet feel on firm ground in my rejection of it. But rejection also has its pain.

Distance is required, even now.

OF A GHASTLY YET USEFUL JOINT ILLNESS, WHICH TEACHETH

*Illness has always been of enormous benefit to me. It might even be
said that I have learned little from anything that did not in some way
make me sick.*

The picture is not an unusual one: A mother and small
child, new to the harshness of the New England winter in one
of the worst flu waves of the century. The mother, flat on her
back with flu, the child, burning with fever. The mother calls
a name someone has given her, a famous pediatrician who
writes for one of the largest of the women's magazines—in
which he reveals himself to be sympathetic, witty, something
of a feminist, even—to be told curtly that she should not call
him at his home at any hour. Furthermore, he does not make
house calls of any kind, and all of this is delivered in the
coldest possible tone.

Still, since he is the only pediatrician she knows of in this
weird place, she drags herself up next morning, when temper-
atures are below zero and a strong wind is blasting off the local
river, and takes the child to see him. He is scarcely less chilly
in person, but, seeing she is black, makes a couple of liberal
comments to put her at her ease. She hates it when his white
fingers touch her child.

A not unusual story. But it places mother and child forever on whichever side of society is opposite this man. She, the
mother, begins to comprehend on deeper levels a story she has
written years before she had a child, of a black mother, very
poor, who, worried to distraction that her child is dying and
no doctor will come to save him, turns to an old folk remedy
for his illness, "strong horse tea." Which is to say, horse urine.
The child dies, of course.

Now too the mother begins to see new levels in the stories

she is at that moment—dizzy with fever—constructing. Why, she says, slapping her forehead, all history is current; all injustice continues on some level, somewhere in the world. "Progress" affects few. Only revolution can affect many.

It was during this same period when, risen from her bed of pain, her child well again and adapting to the cold, that the mother understood that her child, a victim of society as much as she herself—and more of one because as yet she was unable to cross the street without a guiding hand—was in fact the very least of her obstacles in her chosen work. This was brought home to her by the following experience, which, sickening as it was, yet produced in her several desired and ultimately healthful results—one of which was the easy ability to dismiss all people who thought and wrote as if she, herself, did not exist. By "herself" she of course meant multitudes, of which she was at any given time in history, a mere representative.

Our young mother had designed a course in black women writers which she proceeded to teach at an upper-class, largely white, women's college (her students were racially mixed). There she shared an office with a white woman feminist scholar who taught poetry and literature. This woman thought black literature consisted predominantly of Nikki Giovanni, whom she had, apparently, once seen inadvertently on tv. Our young mother was appalled. She made a habit of leaving books by Gwendolyn Brooks, Margaret Walker, Toni Morrison, Nella Larson, Paule Marshall, and Zora Neale Hurston face up on her own desk, which was just behind the white feminist scholar's. For the truly scholarly feminist, she thought, subtlety is enough. She had heard that this scholar was writing a massive study of women's imagination throughout the centuries, and what women's imaginations were better than those displayed on her desk, Our Mother wondered, what woman's imagination better than her own, for that matter; but she was modest, and as I have said, trusted to subtlety.

Time passed. The scholarly tome was published. Dozens of imaginative women paraded across its pages. They were all white. Papers of the status quo, like the *Times,* and liberal inquirers like the *New York Review of Books* and the *Village Voice,* and even feminist magazines such as *Ms.* (for which our young mother was later to work) actually reviewed this work with various degrees of seriousness. Yet to our young mother, the index alone was sufficient proof that the work could not be really serious scholarship, only serious white female chauvinism. And for this she had little time and less patience.

In the prologue to her book The Female Imagination, *Patricia Meyer Spacks attempts to explain why her book deals solely with women in the "Anglo-American literary tradition." She means, of course,* white *women in the Anglo-American tradition. Speaking of the books she has chosen to study, she writes: "Almost all delineate the lives of white, middle-class women. Phyllis Chesler has remarked, 'I have no theory to offer of Third World female psychology in America. As a white woman, I'm reluctant and unable to construct theories about experiences I haven't had.' So am I: the books I talk about describe familiar experience, belong to a familiar cultural setting; their particular immediacy depends partly on these facts. My bibliography balances works everyone knows* (Jane Eyre, Middlemarch) *with works that should be better known* (The Story of Mary MacLane). *Still, the question remains: Why only these?"*

Why only these? Because they are white, and middle class, and because to Spacks, female imagination is only that—a limitation that even white women must find restrictive. Perhaps, however, this is the white female imagination, one that is "reluctant and unable to construct theories about experiences I haven't had." Yet Spacks never lived in nineteenth-century Yorkshire, so why theorize about the Brontës?

It took viewing The Dinner Party, *a feminist statement in art by Judy Chicago, to illuminate—as art always will—the problem. In 1973 when her book* Through the Flower *was published, I was astonished, after reading it, to realize she knew nothing of black women painters. Not even that they exist. I was gratified therefore to learn that in* The Dinner Party *there was a place "set," as it were, for black women. The illumination came when I stood in front of it.*

All the other plates are creatively imagined vaginas (even the one that looks like a piano and the one that bears a striking resemblance to a head of lettuce: and of course the museum guide flutters about talking of "butterflies"!). The Sojourner Truth plate is the only one in the collection that shows—instead of a vagina—a face. In fact, three faces. One, weeping (a truly clichéd tear), which "personifies" the black woman's "oppression," and another, screaming (a no less clichéd scream) with little ugly pointed teeth, "her heroism," and a third, in gimcracky "African" design, smiling; as if the African woman, pre-American slavery, or even today, had no woes. (There is of course a case to be made for being "personified" by a face rather than by a vagina, but that is not what this show is about.)

It occurred to me that perhaps white women feminists, no less than white women generally, cannot imagine black women have vaginas. Or if they can, where imagination leads them is too far to go.

However, to think of black women as women is impossible if you cannot imagine them with vaginas. Sojourner Truth certainly had a vagina, as note her lament about her children, born of her body, but sold into slavery. Note her comment (straightforward, not bathetic) that "when she cried out with a mother's grief, none but Jesus" heard her. Surely a vagina has to be acknowledged when one reads these words. (A vagina the color of raspberries and blackberries—or scup-

*pernongs and muscadines—and of that strong, silvery sweetness, with
as well a sharp flavor of salt).*

And through that vagina, children.

*Perhaps it is the black woman's children, whom the white
woman—having more to offer her own children, and certainly not
having to offer them slavery or a slave heritage or poverty or hatred,
generally speaking: segregated schools, slum neighborhoods, the worst
of everything—resents. For they must always make her feel guilty. She
fears knowing that black women want the best for their children just
as she does. But she also knows black children are to have less in this
world so that her children, white children, will have more. (In some
countries, all.)*

*Better then to deny that the black woman has a vagina. Is capa-
ble of motherhood. Is a woman.*

So, Our Mother* thought, cradling her baby with one
hand, while grading student papers with the other (she found
teaching extremely compatible with child care) the forces of
the opposition are in focus. Fortunately, she had not once
believed that all white women who called themselves feminists
were any the less racist, because work after ambitious work
issued from the country's presses, and, with but a few shining
examples (and Our Mother considered Tillie Olsen's *Silences*
the *most* shining) white women feminists revealed themselves
as incapable as white and black men of comprehending black-
ness and feminism in the same body, not to mention within
the same imagination. By the time Ellen Moers's book on
great *Literary Women* was published in 1976—with Lorraine
Hansberry used as a token of what was not to be included, even
in the future, in women's literature—Our Mother was well

---

* *I am indebted to the African writer Ama Ata Aidoo for my sense of the use-
fulness of the phrase "Our Mother," after reading sections of her novel, then in progress,* Our Sister Killjoy, or Reflections from a Black-eyed Squint.

again. Exchanges like the following, which occurred wherever she was invited to lecture, she handled with aplomb:

White student feminist: "Do you think black women artists should work in the black community?"

Our Mother: "At least for a period in their lives. Perhaps a couple of years, just to give back some of what has been received."

White student feminist: "But if you say that black women should work in the black community, you are saying that race comes before sex. What about black *feminists?* Should *they* be expected to work in the black community? And if so, isn't this a betrayal of their feminism? Shouldn't they work with women?"

Our Mother: "But of course black people come in both sexes."

(Pause, while largely white audience, with sprinkle of perplexed blacks, ponders this possibility.)*

* *(In the preface to Ellen Moers's book* Literary Women: The Great Writers, *she writes: "Just as we are now trying to make sense of women's literature in the great feminist decade of the 1790s, when Mary Wollstonecraft blazed and died, and when, also Mme de Stael came to England and Jane Austen came of age, so the historians of the future will try to order women's literature of the 1960s and 1970s. They will have to consider Sylvia Plath as a woman writer and as a poet; but what will they make of her contemporary compatriot, the playwright Lorraine Hansberry? Born two years before Plath, and dead two years after her in her early thirties, Hansberry was not a suicide but a victim of cancer; she eloquently affirmed life, as Plath brilliantly wooed death.* Historians of the future will undoubtedly be satisfied with the title of Lorraine Hansberry's posthumous volume (named not by Hansberry, but by her former husband who became executor of her estate), *To Be Young, Gifted and Black;* and they will talk of her admiration for Thomas Wolfe; but of Sylvia Plath they will have to say "young, gifted, *and a woman."* [Italics mine].

It is, apparently, inconvenient, if not downright mind straining, for white women scholars to think of black women as women, perhaps because "woman" (like

OF OUR MOTHER'S CONTINUED PILGRIMAGE TOWARD TRUTH AT
THE EXPENSE OF VAIN PRIDE, OR: ONE MORE RIVER TO CROSS

*It was a river she did not even know was there. Hence her dif-
ficulty in crossing it.*

Our Mother was glad, during the period of the above revelations—all eventually salutary to her mental health—to have
occasion to address a large group of educated and successful
black women. She had adequate respect for both education and
success, since both were often needed, she thought, to comprehend the pains and anxieties of women who have neither. She
spoke praisingly of Black Herstory, she spoke as she often did,
deliberately of her mother (formerly missing from both literature and history); she spoke of the alarming rise in the suicide
of young black women all over America. She asked that these
black women address themselves to this crisis. Adddress themselves, in effect, to themselves.

Our Mother was halted in mid-speech. She was told she
made too much of Black Herstory. That she should not assume
her mother represented poor mothers all over the world (which
she did assume) and, furthermore, she was told, those to address were black men; that, though it appeared more black

*"man" among white males) is a name they are claiming for themselves, and themselves
alone. Racism decrees that if they are now women (years ago they were ladies, but
fashions change) then black women must, perforce, be something else. (While they were
"ladies" black women could be "women," and so on.)*

*In any case, Moers expects "historians of the future" to be as dense as those in the
past, and at least as white. It does not occur to her that they might be white women
with a revolutionary rather than a reactionary or liberal approach to literature, let
alone black women. Yet many are bound to be. Those future historians, working-class
black and white women, should have no difficulty comprehending: "Lorraine Hansberry: Young, Gifted, Black, Activist, Woman, Eloquent Affirmer of Life," and:
"Sylvia Plath: Young, Gifted, White, Non-Activist Woman (in fact, fatally self-
centered), Brilliant Wooer of Death."*

women than men were committing suicide, still everyone knew black women to be the stronger of these two. Those women who committed suicide were merely sick, apparently with an imaginary or in any case a causeless disease. Furthermore, Our Mother was told, "Our men must be supported in every way, *whatever they do.*" Since so many of "our men" were doing little at the time but denigrating black women (and especially such educated and "successful" black women as those assembled) when they deigned to recognize them at all, and since this denigration and abandonment was a direct cause of at least some of the suicides, Our Mother was alarmed. Our Mother was furious. Our Mother burst into tears (which some around her thought a really strong black woman would not do).

However, Our Mother did not for one moment consider becoming something other than black and female. She was in the condition of twin "afflictions" for life. And, to tell the truth, she rather enjoyed being more difficult things in one lifetime than anybody else. She even regretted (at times) not being still desperately poor. She regretted (at times) her private sexual behavior was so much her own business it was in no sense provocative. She was, in her own obstacle-crazed way, a snob.

But it was while recuperating from this blow to her complete trust in *all* black women (which was foolish, as all categorical trust is, of course) that she began to understand a simple principle. People do not wish to appear foolish; to avoid the appearance of foolishness, they were willing to remain actually fools. This led directly to a clearer grasp of many black women's attitudes about the women's movement.

They had seen, perhaps earlier than she (she was notorious for her optimism regarding any progressive group effort) that

white feminists are very often indistinguishable in their attitudes from any other white persons in America. She did not
blame white *feminists* for the overturned buses of schoolchildren from Baton Rouge to Boston, as many black women did,
or for the black schoolchildren beaten and spat upon. But
look, just look, at the recent exhibit of women painters at the
Brooklyn Museum!

("Are there no black women painters represented here?"
one asked a white woman feminist.

"It's a *women's* exhibit!" she replied.)

OF THE NEED FOR INTERNATIONALISM, ALIGNMENT WITH
NON-AMERICANS, NON-EUROPEANS, AND NON-CHAUVINISTS AND
AGAINST MALE SUPREMACISTS OR WHITE SUPREMACISTS WHEREVER
THEY EXIST ON THE GLOBE, WITH AN APPRECIATION OF ALL WHITE
AMERICAN FEMINISTS WHO KNOW MORE OF NONWHITE WOMEN'S
HERSTORY THAN "AND AIN'T I A WOMAN" BY SOJOURNER TRUTH

There was never a time when Our Mother thought, when
someone spoke of "the women's movement," that this referred
only to the women's movement in America. When she
thought of women moving, she automatically thought of
women all over the world. She recognized that to contemplate
the American women's movement in isolation from the rest of
the world would be—given the racism, sexism, elitism, and
ignorance of so many American feminists—extremely defeat-
ing of solidarity among women as well as depressing to the
most optimistic spirit. Our Mother had traveled and had every
reason to understand that women's freedom was an idea whose
time had come, an idea sweeping the world.

The women of China "hold up half the sky." They, who
once had feet the size of pickles. The women of Cuba, fighting
the combined oppression of African and Spanish macho, know
that their revolution will be "shit" if they are the ones to do
the laundry, dishes, and floors after working all day, side by

side in factory and field with their men, "making the revolution." The women of Angola, Mozambique, and Eritrea have picked up the gun and propped against it demand their right to fight the enemy within as the enemy without their countries. The enemy within is the patriarchal system that has kept women virtual slaves throughout memory.

Our Mother understood that in America, white women who are truly feminist (for whom racism is inherently an impossibility, as long as some black people can also be conceived of as women) are largely outnumbered by *average* American white women for whom racism, inasmuch as it assures white privilege, is an accepted way of life. Naturally, many of these women, to be trendy, will leap to the feminist banner because it is now the place to be seen. What was required of women of color, many of whom have, over the centuries, and with the best of reasons, become racialists if not racists themselves, was to learn to distinguish between who was the real feminist and who was not, and to exert energy in feminist collaborations only when there is little risk of wasting it. The rigors of this discernment will invariably keep throwing women of color back upon themselves, where there is, indeed, so much work, of a feminist nature, to be done. From the stamping out of clitoridectomy and "female circumcision" in large parts of Arabia and Africa, to the heating of freezing urban tenements in which poor mothers and children are trapped alone to freeze to death. From the encouragement of women artists in Latin America to the founding of feminist publications for women of color in North America. From the stopping of pornography, child slavery, and forced prostitution and molestation of minors in the home and in Times Square, to the defense of women beaten and raped each Saturday night the world over by their husbands.

To the extent that black women disassociate themselves

from the women's movement, they abandon their responsibilities to women throughout the world. This is a serious abdication from and misuse of radical black herstorical tradition: Harriet Tubman, Sojourner, Ida B. Wells, and Fannie Lou Hamer would not have liked it. Nor do I.

From my journal: Jackson, Mississippi, June 15, 1972:
   R said today: "I can cook soup, and eggs, and windows!."
   She also said, while drawing letters on the kitchen table: "A, D, and O." Then, "Oh-oh, the O is upside down!"

I feel very little guilt (most days) about the amount of time "taken from my daughter" by my work. I was amazed to discover I could read a book and she could exist at the same time. And how soon she learned that there are other things to enjoy besides myself. Between an abstracted, harassed adult and an affectionate sitter or neighbor's child who can be encouraged to return a ball, there is no contest, as one knows.

There *was* a day, when, finally after five years of writing *Meridian* (a book "about" the civil rights movement, feminism, socialism, the shakiness of revolutionaries and the radicalization of saints—the kind of book out of the political sixties that white feminist scholar Francine du Plessix Gray declared recently in the *New York Times Book Review* did not exist) I felt a pang.

I wrote this self-pitying poem:

> Now that the book is finished,
> now that I know my characters will live,
> I can love my child again.
> She need sit no longer
> at the back of my mind
> the lonely sucking of her thumb
> a giant stopper in my throat.

But this was as much celebration as anything. After all, the book *was* finished, the characters *would* live, and of course I'd loved my daughter all along. As for "the giant stopper in my throat," perhaps it is the fear of falling silent, *mute,* writers have from time to time. This fear is a hazard of the work itself, which requires a *severity* toward the self that is often overwhelming in its discomfort, more than it is the existence of one's child, who, anyway, by the age of seven, at the latest, is one's friend, and can be told of the fears one has, that she can, by listening to one, showing one a new dance step, perhaps, sharing a coloring book, or giving one a hug, help allay.

In any case, it is not my child who tells me I have no femaleness white women must affirm. Not my child who says I have no rights black men or black women must respect.

It is not my child who has purged my face from history and herstory and left mystory just that, a mystery; my child loves my face and would have it on every page, if she could, as I have loved my own parents' faces above all others, and have refused to let them be denied, or myself to let them go.

Not my child, who in a way *beyond* all this, but really of a piece with it, destroys the planet daily, and has begun on the universe.

We are together, my child and I. Mother and child, yes, but *sisters* really, against whatever denies us all that we are.

For a long time I had this sign, which I constructed myself, deliberately, out of false glitter, over my desk:

Dear Alice,

> Virginia Woolf had madness;
> George Eliot had ostracism,
> somebody else's husband,

and did not dare to use
her own name.
Jane Austen had no privacy
and no love life.
The Brontë sisters never went anywhere
and died young
and dependent on their father.
Zora Hurston (ah!) had no money
and poor health.

You have R—who is
much more delightful
and less distracting
than any of the calamities
above.

INGRID BENGIS

The Middle Period

Quite often, when I am living through one or another form of "hard times," I think . . . no, I don't want to be a writer anymore . . . no, I can't bear the isolation, the uncertainty, the financial insecurity, the constant wrestling with inner truths, the constant necessity for keeping my eyes open to life, the unabating pressure to push myself beyond what I have only just begun to master, the sense that there is, in this, the most unpredicatable of professions, no resting place.

When these thoughts and feelings come over me (and they arrive not infrequently), I am quick to invent a new career for myself: chef, psychotherapist, lobsterfisherwoman, diamond cutter, filmmaker, each of which, from a distance, appears to combine in its own way the intensity and symbolic weight and singularity of being a writer with none of its disadvantages. As a diamond cutter, I am part of a highly specialized working community, involved in the transformation of a lump of matter into an aesthetic object universally recognized for its value. I have a useful, financially stable trade and participate in an activity that engages a broad spectrum of society, from miners to merchants, Hasidim, movie stars, Irish, Puerto Rican, Jewish, and Wasp brides, old moneyed families, and royalty. As a chef and master of culinary aesthetics, I move back and forth between my two preferred environments: the marketplace and the kitchen. As a therapist, I work with the same intensity as a writer but deal with the inner lives of others rather than with myself. I see specific results. I am not alone. As a lobster-fisherwoman, I am alone, but nonetheless part of a tight interdependent community, daily testing myself against nature in its purest form.

These fantasies have been very important to me, giving me an imaginative freedom that I rarely possess otherwise, providing me with a momentary breath of fresh air, releasing me from the sometimes claustrophobic intensity my own work engenders. But at the moment when it becomes necessary for me to do anything about them, I always balk. For each new imagined career, even as it is stimulating me, is raising a dread specter as well . . . that if I became too deeply involved with it, I might stop being a writer. This prospect pitches me headlong into such an acute state of anxiety that I instantly discard all of my career fantasies, resolving to protect at all costs that vast inner space in which everything I write is obliged to germinate. I will do nothing, I say to myself, rather than distract myself . . . even from the writing which I may not, at the time, be doing.

It thus has become apparent to me that the counterpart of

my career fantasy is a career dread, a fear of doing anything at all that might jeopardize my writing. It was the dread that made me choose to support my writing with work as a waitress or taxi driver or temporary secretary, rather than as a publicist or television scriptwriter, because I was afraid of losing the ability to discriminate between real work and hack work, and because I wanted the freedom to drop whatever I was doing at a moment's notice if luck or inspiration raised its imperial head. It was the dread that made me isolate myself at my house in Maine for months at a time, convinced that any contact or conversation would dilute the force of my writing; the dread that made me alternately determined to share my life fully with someone I loved, and terrified that if I did so, happiness might prevent me from creating. It was the dread that made me decide that I could not have children (although I desperately wanted a child), made me shun intellectuals for fear that too much cerebral conversation would dull the force of my instinct, and drove me into acute and often painful solitudes. Ultimately, it was the dread as well that made me abandon my own ascetic and aestheticized criteria and rush headlong into experience all over again, because it seemed that I had taken the worst risk of all: that of removing myself from life, and therefore having nothing to say.

Having jammed the gears into reverse, I promptly took on the world. I became the legal guardian of a twelve-year-old homeless child and brought her from Maine to New York, deciding to give her the best of everything on my income of $8,000 a year; I fell into a complicated love; I settled into Manhattan and an unmanageable debt; I worked full time as a secretary and was able to do almost no writing at all; I lost the child. In short, I went from being a writer who protected my sacred solitude with vehement determination to being a woman so deeply entangled in life's common and uncommon dilemmas that I could scarcely juggle them all, let alone detach myself long enough to extract their meaningful literary essence.

Thus, for almost two years, I mistakenly considered myself "blocked." I wrote a few articles, part of an unpublished novella, and a few incomplete short stories. On the one hand, I had rejected the Himalayan purity that I associated with being a writer, and possibly, rejected even writing itself. On the other, I guessed that I might be rejecting only what had already rejected me. Because I could not work anymore, I thought that I never would again. Not until the summer of 1978, when I finally began working on a new novel, did I realize I had bought a literary suit that was much too large for me and had spent the last years trying to grow into it.

At the age of thirty-five, I have just begun to become the kind of person who could understand the kind of book I would want to write. As a young woman writer I took it for granted that I was at the center of the universe; as a somewhat older woman writer I found life scarily impartial to my own hardly unique difficulties. Having lost the literal and literary sense of myself as an outsider who, while frequently misunderstood, is ultimately triumphant, I gained the knowledge that I was part of the human race. En route, I learned something about the tendrils of affection that wrap themselves around one so insistently that ultimately no choices or decisions can be made without taking them into consideration; something about the possibilities and responsibilities of motherhood; something about love that is other than romantic; something about success and the irregularity of the creative process; something about the entanglements of money, inflation, and debt. When my father developed terminal cancer, and I had to watch his long slow deterioration, I also learned something about the trauma of age and dying.

That is a lot to learn in a few years. And it is a lot more to translate into literature. During the time when I was not actively writing but rather living, and trying to untangle the themes that seemed to be emerging from my own life and my collisions with the lives of others, I was frequently obsessed with my inability to write. If someone asked, "Are you working on anything?" I answered "no" with the same defensive embarrassment I had exhibited years ago when people asked me, "Are you married?" and I answered, "No, just living together." "No, we're just living together, me and this seed of an unborn book. We're not ready yet to put it in writing."

But while we lived together (this seed of a book and I), it changed and I changed. By the time I sat down at the typewriter, I was writing a book quite unlike the one I had at first planned to write, because I was quite unlike the person who had first considered writing it. I had an altered vision of life, not to mention an altered life. My experiences had compelled me to start thinking about the ways in which life changes character and capacity, the ways in which the accidents of success or failure influence one's sense of oneself, the ways in which society both creates and destroys the human capacity for survival. Although I had always been inspired by the delicate balancing act required for one person to understand another, even under the best of circumstances, my concerns when I was in my twenties focused primarily upon the way in which such communication evaporates in the language used by men and women. Now, in my thirties, I find myself less preoccupied with men and women per se and more concerned with the obstacles to understanding that divide generations, classes, layers of society . . . those who live close to the bone of survival and those who are padded from it by the protective flesh of inexperience or privilege or "normality."

What I want to do is nab something of life in motion. All too frequently, however, the shape of the sentences elude me, the tone of voice for them eludes me, the characters who will be strong enough in themselves to bear the weight of what is on my mind elude me. What remains undone is what art can do when it lays its light hand on the heavy materials of life. I know that although the passion for communication drove me to become a writer in the first place, passion does not always guarantee progeny. I am impatient with myself, annoyed that it is taking so long, that I cannot yet capture even the shadow of what I have begun to see. But it may be that I will have to settle for nothing less than a full-term pregnancy.

I was nine years old when I started writing poems, twelve when I began creating tragic stories—one about an old woman, abandoned by her children and reduced to begging in the streets, another about a woman left in a remote farmhouse by her husband, and a third about a child overhearing a quarrel between her parents on her sixth birthday. Only now am I beginning to realize that the thematic crosscurrents that preoccupied me then are the same as those with which I am struggling now. Except then, I saw them with the eyes of a child, and now I am trying to see them with the eyes of an adult.

I have always been magnetized by people under stress. What will they do when pressed beyond their habitual circumstances? What will I do? Will they prove themselves larger than themselves or smaller? Will I? What happens to the human personality when it is faced with the raw, intractable materials of life? These questions have formed a kind of pattern of obsession, in which my own life has become the testing ground for various forms of courage and endurance, in an attempt (at first consciously pursued, and later reflexive) to break through the barriers of my own limitations.

This testing took multiple forms, challenging not only my physical courage but my emotional stamina. As a child, I used to force myself to stay in the room when my parents fought, trying, by sheer strength of will, to divide myself cleanly enough in half that I would be capable of entering fully into their separate souls and loving them both equally. As a fifteen-year-old, I stood in the secret hazing rooms of Phi Delta sorority and refused to talk dirty about my friends, even though my sorority sisters kept hissing, "We're going to break your pride, Bengis, just wait, we're going to break your pride." As a young adult, I bent down at high noon in the tomato fields of an Israeli desert kibbutz and picked tomatoes until I fainted and had to be carried to a cool room; two hours later, I returned to the field and started picking again, though this time I did not faint and got my first glimmering of what it meant to distinguish bravery from foolishness. As a woman of thirty-one, I took on the raising of someone else's child. Dating from the child's arrival in my life, I stopped looking for the hardships that would challenge my endurance and began understanding that courage, far from being a dramatically active pursuit, was instead a passive, frequently invisible aspect of existence, without which none of us would survive at all. This courage, so subtle and various in its most authentic forms that it most often passes unnoticed, has become one of my primary concerns. And my awareness of it has changed, to a degree that I cannot yet estimate, both my life and my work.

She first appeared when I was midway through my first novel. At that point, I had been living alone for several years, and my life, although vividly compressed in my first book, was, in actual fact, chaste, solitary and still. I had recently passed the red flag of my thirtieth birthday, and two fresh currents of feeling had begun to converge in me: the first was a fear that after I finished writing this novel, I would have nothing more to say, and the second was a sense that the world that I had so far described in my work was notably circumscribed by absorption in myself and the trials of the inner life. I was, although not exactly bored with the inner life, nonetheless conscious that, in literature, it had its limitations. I was also conscious that living alone lent itself to such absorptions, since one's dialogues are most frequently with oneself, and the self becomes the fixed pole around which one's ideas and feelings whirl. I was tired of my highly touted freedom, tired of adventures, tired of a certain kind of courage that was beginning to seem shallow to me. I felt that my commitments were too few and too sparse. I craved responsibility. But not the responsibility of artificially attaching myself to some new cause. What I wanted was a responsibility that would extend, in a straight line, from my soul to the soul of another. What I wanted was motherhood.

And I got it, though not in the form I had anticipated. An abandoned Maine child from the island where I have a house found me, and I found her. Her family situation was staggeringly complex, but in the end, it added up to something quite simple: she had no place to live. So she moved in with me, and after a year, a judge appointed me her legal guardian with a recommendation of full adoption. Suddenly I had the daughter I had always wanted, a ten-year-old waif with more savvy about the hard realities of life than any child I had ever known, and less schooling than the State of Maine deemed acceptable. I say "my daughter," because that is what she was, and in some way, still is, to me, despite the fact that a year ago she returned to Maine to live with her natural mother. My daughter because she stirred up in me that fierce protectiveness and occasional blindness that are the home territory of most mothers; my daughter because the love I felt for her was only matched by my frustration over raising her; my daughter because, no matter how hard things became with her (and they eventually became extremely hard), it would never have occurred to me to let go of her.

In the process of living with her, I learned not only what it meant to be a single parent raising a child on a limited income but also what it meant to love another human being as much as I had, until then, loved only myself. I learned that there are more things influencing the shape and direction of a life than I had ever imagined. And because living with a child forces you into society, I learned a great deal about the myriad social demands and pressures, the myriad human variables that invisibly but powerfully control individual daily existence. I learned what a vast and complex thing is an ordinary life. I also learned what my limitations were as a writer.

Before the child moved in with me, I was blessed with a certain naïve optimism about the future, or rather, about my ability to control the future. Even though I was in financial difficulties at the time of her arrival, I assumed that those difficulties were temporary, and that my new book, scheduled for publication in a few months, would change what I then thought of as my "present circumstances." Thus, several months after I had been appointed her guardian, I brought her to New York and decided to enroll her in a small private school with a tuition I could not afford. Because her education had been so spotty, and her needs for individual attention were so great, a private school seemed to be not *an* alternative but the only alternative. Never having overextended myself financially before, I had no conception of the possible consequences of my decision.

But the new book was not a success. Quietly at first, and then not so quietly, I went broke, and was stunned to discover that once again, as in the days before the appearance of my first book, I could not support myself through my writing. Except this time, there was a difference: this time I was thirty-two, not twenty-two. Mobility and improvisation had ceased to be the guiding principles of my life. Whereas driving a taxi or working as a waitress had been inspired acts of self-preservation when I was younger, they now seemed to signal not the occasion for a sense of élan but a future of anticipated defeat. Not only that, but this time I had a child. This time, I was not just devising a means of support for myself and writing "on the side" or "in between." There was no "in between." Within a very short time, it became painfully clear to me just how much of a difference that represented. It was the difference between bohemianism and that mind-boggling state in which absolutely every decision, from the smallest to the largest, involves a strenuous effort to produce money one doesn't have . . . money used not to gain one's freedom but to ensure one's survival. Suddenly, I found myself confronted with a kind of desperation I had never known before. On one side, I was wedged in by escalating necessities, on the other constrained by rapidly diminishing alternatives. It was under these circumstances that I went out and took a job as a temporary secretary, which gave me a reliable, if excruciatingly small, income and preserved for me the illusion (to which I continued clinging) that this "state of affairs" was temporary and would eventually sort itself out.

In the meantime, I struggled unsuccessfully to pay my

child's tuition, because I thought that moving her from one school to another in the middle of the term would create more problems than it would solve, struggled to pay a rent that had become exorbitant, because I felt that moving again would jeopardize her nascent sense of stability, struggled to sever the ties that bound her too tightly to her own past, and struggled, in scattered moments of clarity, to write my way out of my difficulties by conferring upon them an aesthetic that would order my experiences even if it could not directly alter them.

Increasingly, I began to feel that my life, which only a few years earlier had seemed painfully one-dimensional, had become so weighted with multiple necessities that it was impossible for me to stand still long enough to focus on them. If isolation had divorced me from the external realities of life, commitment was now divorcing me from the possibilities for solitude, reflection, and creation. By the end of a work day, I was far too exhausted to scan my own interior with the detached objectivity of an encephalogram, far too bound by immediate problems to perceive the clear middle distance beyond them.

On the one hand, I grew resentful that life, which until then had spared many of my most sensitive feelings, seemed unwilling to respond to my exhortations that it should be "better" or "easier" or less complicated. On the other hand, however, I became oddly grateful for being compelled finally to destroy in myself some of these illusions that until then had made it possible for me to construct both a private and a literary universe based on desire rather than necessity. For if human life was, by and large, governed by necessity, then why should mine be uniquely exempt? And if it was exempt, then how could I ever understand what it meant to be anything other than adolescent?

By the time the child left, I felt as if I had aged ten years rather than two. During much of the time when she lived with me, I had been both stifled and overwhelmed by the sheer effort of trying to master a seemingly unassimilable volume of experience. During the period after her departure, I felt no less overwhelmed. Having discovered that responsibility, no matter how difficult or painful, was what gave my life depth and meaning and resonance, I suddenly found myself with no one to be responsible for. Obliged to perceive life differently while she was with me, it was impossible for me to turn back and become once again the young woman I had been before she entered my life. If anything, I had to burrow more deeply into my sense of what that responsibility meant, had to know finally what it was to have one's roots inextricably entangled in the lives of others.

A year later, I am still burrowing. The questions that her presence in my life forced me to raise have not disappeared. They have instead acquired that intensity which so often defines a transforming experience sharply marked by a beginning and an end. And she, as a result, has become larger than life. I know that if I wish to bring her back to size, I can only do so by a kind of literary transfusion, in which the blood of the life I shared with her is pumped into an invented someone else, a someone who may not superficially resemble her at all but whom I will nonetheless recognize as her legitimate heir. No matter what the subject, the subject is always love.

TONI CADE BAMBARA

What It Is I Think
I'm Doing Anyhow

Winter 1979. We are now in the fourth year of the last quarter of the twentieth century. And the questions that face the millions of us on the earth are—in whose name will the twenty-first century be claimed? Can the planet be rescued from the psychopaths? Where are the evolved, poised-for-light adepts who will assume the task of administering power in a human interest, of redefining power as being not the privilege or class right to define, deform, and dominate but as the human responsibility to define, transform, and develop?

The previous quarter-century, from 1950 to 1975, was an era hallmarked by revolution, a period in which we experienced a radical shift in the political-power configurations of the globe. The current quarter, from 1976 to 2,000, is also

153

characterized by revolution, a period in which we are awakening to and experiencing a profound change in the psychic-power configurations of the globe.

There is a war going on and a transformation taking place. That war is not simply the contest between the socialist camp and the capitalist camp over which political/economic/social arrangement will enjoy hegemony in the world, nor is it simply the battle over turf and resources. Truth is one of the issues in this war. The truth, for example, about inherent human nature, about our potential, our agenda as earth people, our destiny.

Writing is one of the ways I participate in struggle—one of the ways I help to keep vibrant and resilient that vision that has kept the Family going on. Through writing I attempt to celebrate the tradition of resistance, attempt to tap Black potential, and try to join the chorus of voices that argues that exploitation and misery are neither inevitable nor necessary. Writing is one of the ways I participate in the transformation—one of the ways I practice the commitment to explore bodies of knowledge for the usable wisdoms they yield. In writing, I hope to encourage the fusion of those disciplines whose split (material science versus metaphysics versus aesthetics versus politics versus . . .) predisposes us to accept fragmented truths and distortions as the whole. Writing is one of the ways I do my work in the world.

There are no career labels for that work, no facile terms to describe the tasks of it. Suffice to say that I do not take lightly the fact that I am on the earth at this particular time in human history, and am here as a member of a particular soul group and of a particular sex, having this particular adventure as a Pan-Africanist-socialist-feminist in the United States. I figure all that means something—about what I'm here to understand and to do.

Of all the mothers in the world I might have been born to, I was born at a particular moment to mine and to no other. As a kid with an enormous appetite for knowledge and a gift for imagining myself anywhere in the universe, I always seemed to be drawn to the library or to some music spot or to 125th Street and Seventh Avenue, Speaker's Corner, to listen to Garveyites, Father Diviners, Rastafarians, Muslims, trade unionists, communists, Pan-Africanists. And when I recall the host of teachers who have crossed my path and always right on time, so unfull of shit, so unlike the terrified and lost salaried teachers in the schools—and not only that, but having managed to survive Mather Academy boarding school's diet to come of age in the sixties—and all the while having some swamphag all up in my face asking me about my dreams (have I had a vision yet, have the voices given me instructions yet)—certainly it all means something. This is, after all, not a comic book. It's my life. So I pay attention. And I understand that I am being groomed to perform particular work in this world. Writing is one of the ways I try to do it.

The old folks say, "It's not how little we know that hurts so, but that so much of what we know ain't so." As a mother, teacher, writer, community worker, neighbor, I am concerned about accurate information, verifiable facts, sound analyses, responsible research, principled study, and people's assessment of the meaning of their lives. I'm interested in usable truths. Which means rising above my training, thinking better than I've been taught, developing a listening habit, making the self available to intelligence, engaging in demystification, and seeking out teachers at every turn. In many respects the writings are notebooks I'm submitting to those teachers for examination. There have been a host of teachers. Once I thought anyone with enthusiasm about information was a good teacher. Then, anyone with an analysis of this country who could help illuminate the condition, status, and process of the Family, who could help me decide how to put my wrath and my skills to the service of folks who sustain me. Later, anyone who could throw open the path and lead me back to the ancient wisdoms was teacher. In more recent times, any true dialectician (material/spiritual) who could increase my understanding of all, I say all, the forces afoot in the universe was teacher. I'm entering my forties with more simplistic criteria—anyone with a greater capacity for love than I is a valuable teacher. And when I look back on the body of book reviews I've produced in the past fifteen years, for all their socioideolitero brilliant somethinorother, the underlying standard always seemed to be—Does this author here genuinely love his/her community?

The greatest challenge in writing, then, in the earlier stages was to strike a balance between candor, honesty, integrity, and truth—terms that are fairly synonomous for crossword puzzlers and thesaurus ramblers but hard to equate as living actions. Speaking one's mind, after all, does not necessarily mean one is in touch with the truth or even with the facts. Being honest and frank in terms of my own where—where I'm at at a given point in my political/spiritual/etc. development—is not necessarily in my/our interest to utter, not necessarily in the interest of health, wholesomeness. Certain kinds of poisons, for example—rage, bitterness, revenge—don't need to be in the atmosphere, not to mention in my mouth. I don't, for example, hack up racists and stuff them in metaphorical boxes. I do not wish to lend them energy, for one thing. Though certainly there are "heavies" that people my stories. But I don't, for example, conjure up characters for the express purpose of despising them, of breaking their humps in public. I used to be astounded at Henry James et al., so nice nasty about it too, soooo refined. Gothic is of no interest to me. I try not to lend energy to building grotesqueries, depicting morbid relationships, dramatizing perversity. Folks come up to me 'lowing as how since I am a writer I would certainly want to hear blah, blah, blah, blah. They dump shit all over me, tell me about every ugly overheard and lived-through nightmare imaginable. They've got the wrong writer. The kid can't use it. I straightaway refer them to the neighborhood healer, certain that anyone so intoxicated would surely welcome a cleansing. But they persist—"Hey, this is for real, square business. The truth." I don't doubt that the horror tales are factual. I don't even doubt that ugly is a truth for somebody . . . somehow. But I'm not convinced that ugly is *the* truth that can save us, redeem us. The old folks teach that. Be triflin' and ugly and they say, "Deep down, gal, you know that ain't right," appealing to a truth about our deep-down nature. Good enough for me. Besides, I can't get happy writing ugly weird. If I'm not laughing while I work, I conclude that I am not communicating nourishment, since laughter is the most sure-fire healant I know. I don't know all my readers, but I know well for whom I write. And I want for them no less than I want for myself—wholesomeness.

It all sounds so la-di-da and tra-la-la. I can afford to be sunny. I'm but one voice in the chorus. The literature(s) of our time are a collective effort, dependent on so many views, on so many people's productions. I am frequently asked to name my favorite writer, or the one writer who best captures the Black experience, or the one sister who is really doing it. What can I do but crack up and stuff another carrot in the juicer? No way in the world I can swing over to that frame of reference so dominated by solo-voice thinking. Given the range of experiences available to a soul having the human adventure in this time and place, given that we have just begun to tap the limitless reservoir of cultural, societal, global, possibilities. Hell, there aren't even phrases in the languages for half the things happening just on the block where I live, not yet anyhow. Who could possibly be this *one* writer that interviewers and reviewers are always harping about? I read everybody I can get to, and I appreciate the way "American literature" is being redefined now that the Black community is dialoguing without defensive postures, now that the Puerto Rican writers are coming through loud and clear, and the Chicano and Chicana writers, and Native American and Asian-American. . . . There's a lot of work to do, a lot of records to get straight, a lot of living to share, a lot to plumb. This reader wants it all—the oddball, the satiric, the grim, the ludicrous, what have you. As for my own writing, I prefer the upbeat. It pleases me to blow three or four choruses of just sheer energetic fun and optimism, even in the teeth of rats, racists, repressive cops, bomb lovers, irresponsibles, murderers. I am convinced, I guess, that everything will be all right.

When I originally drafted the title story of my first story collection, *Gorilla, My Love,* the tone was severe, grim. The confrontations between the kid and the adults who so nonchalantly lie to and de-spirit little kids were raging red. Writing in a rage can produce some interesting pyrotechnics, but there are other ways to keep a fire ablaze, it seems to me. Besides, I know that everything will be O.K. for that little girl, so tough, so compassionate, so brave. Her encounter with the movie manager who put a come-on title on the marquee and then screened another movie altogether, and her encounter with her uncle who promised to marry her when she grew up and then turned right around and married some full-grown woman—those are rehearsals that will hold her in good stead in later encounters with more menacing and insidious people.

That's second of all. First of all, while little kids' lives are most definitely characterized by intense anger over the injustices heaped upon them, it's not an anger that can sustain itself for twelve typewritten pages. Bunny rabbits and new socks and the neighbor kid's skates have a way of distracting kids. So clearly I had to solve a problem in pitch and voice. Once I could grin/cry through it, the writing felt right. Readers seem to laugh through it as well, as I've observed on subways, in laundromats, in libraries, and classrooms. And the lesson is not missed. So, as my classroom experience as a teacher has taught me, there are hipper ways to get to gut and brain than with hot pokers and pincers.

"Broken-Field Running," in the 1977 collection *The Seabirds Are Still Alive,* was more of a challenge. It wasn't so much a problem in pitch as a problem in balancing the elements of mood. I'd been observing architectural changes in my community since the street rebellions. Schools, public housing, parks were being designed in such a way as to wreck community sovereignty, to render it impossible for neighbors to maintain surveillance and security of turf. I was enraged. I wrote a blazing essay on the subject, snarling, shooting from both hips. Hadn't a clue as to how to finish it or to whom to send it. Wrote a story instead. The first problem then was balancing the essay voice and the story voice; the second to keep the two dominant emotions of the narrator stabilized, in tension. The story is an odd sort of moody piece about a combatant, a teacher whose faith is slipping, whose belief in the capacity for transformation is splintering. I was trying to get at how difficult it is to maintain the fervent spirit at a time when the Movement is mute, when only a few enclaves exist. The teacher's work, her friend, her training, and most of all her responsibility to the children help to keep her centered, help to keep her in touch with the best of herself. But her task is rough.

Time out to say this—I often read in reviews that my stories are set in the sixties and are nostalgic and reminiscent of days when revolution was believed in. News to me. With the exception of "The Long Night," all the stories in *Seabirds* are in the "right now" time they were drafted. I suppose for too many people the idea that struggle is neither new nor over is hard to grasp, that there is a radical tradition as old as the H.M.S. *Jesus* or whatever that ship was that hauled over the first boatload. Some weeks ago, I read from my new work at a workshop of novels-in-progress. It was an excerpt about an elderly woman recalling the days when she worked for the Sleeping Car Porters and organized Ida B. Wells clubs in Harlem. Two out of three people at the reading assumed that the novel was set in the late sixties and that the woman was talking about the earlier sixties. Gives a person pause. Amnesia is a hellafying thing. The impulse to pronounce the Movement dead ain't no joke either.

Back to "Broken-Field Running." It was spring 1974 and I'd just returned from a rally at which I heard that genocide was a fact in the Colored World, that the struggle was all over cause nobody cared anymore and blah, blah, blah, blah, accompanied by statistics and all the evangelical zeal of the brimstone tent belters. So in that woe-is-us mood, I began work on the story. And before I knew it, my character Lacy had picked it up and run off with it. Even while she was slipping in the snow and so in need of all kinds of support now that the thousands of combatants of a few years ago were/are no longer very visible, she managed to horse around enough to keep the story from getting depressing—depression being, to my mind, a form of collaboration. The kids in her orbit after all, are proof, mandate, motive to keep on keeping on. I guess then, that the message is—and I am a brazenly "message" writer, which seems to unsettle many reviewers—that in periods of high consciousness, one has to build the network and the foundation to sustain one through periods of high conflict and low consciousness. What goes around, comes around, as folks say.

Of course it is difficult to maintain the faith and keep working toward the new time if you've had no *experience* of it, not *seen* ordinary people actually transform selves and societies. That is the back-and-forth of the story "The Apprentice" in *Seabirds*. The young sister who narrates the story underestimates her own ability to fashion a revolutionary outlook, for she's not seen what my other character, the organizer Naomi, has seen. We, however, know that she will grow. She's got fine spirit for all her caterwauling. And we suspect too, I imagine, that whatever moved her into the circle of community workers and made her an apprentice in the first place will continue to operate, to inform her choices. And too, Naomi is kinda fun to hang out with. And that is the way many join ranks, after all, through an attraction to a given person. It's like the gospel song instructs, "You never know who's watching you," who's taking you as a model. I seem to recall that I invited Naomi onto the scene as a way of answering the grim reapers at that 1974 rally. If you're trying to recruit people to a particular kind of work, the recruiter has to stand for something attractive. I'd be willing to follow Naomi anywhere. She has heart to spare.

I got a lot of mixed reactions about the story "The Organizer's Wife" in *Seabirds*. Feminist types didn't like the title; some said they refused to read the story because the title was such a putdown. Others liked the fact that Virginia, the lead character, kicked the preacher's ass for more reasons than for turning her husband in but, nonetheless, would have been happier had she left town or died in childbirth, by way of my protesting the system. Some letters and calls said I should have had Graham, the organizer, die some gruesome death in that southern jail to protest, etc. Kill Graham off and have Virginia go batty, or leave, or die in childbirth? What kind of message would that have been? How would I have explained that to my daughter? She's looking forward to growing up as a responsibile change agent. I'm well aware that we are under siege, that the system kills, that the terms of race and class war have not altered very much. But death is not a truth that inspires, that pumps up the heart, that mobilizes. It's defeatist to dwell always on the consequences of risks. It's proracist to assume we can't take a chance. I am not interested in collaborating with the program of the forces that systematically underdevelop. So Graham lives and Virginia wakes up.

"The Organizer's Wife," written in 1975 and set in 1975, is a love story, layer after layer. Lovers and combatants are not defeated. That is the message of that story, the theme of the entire collection, the wisdom that gets me up in the morning, honored to be here. It is a usable truth.

I'm reminded of a rip-roaring visit to a couple, friends of mine, who invited me to dinner and began discussing Charles Johnson's wonderful book *Faith and the Good Thing*. Leaning across the table at each other, rattling dishes, knocking over the candlestick, they proceeded to debate with brandished forks whether or not the author's burning up of a baby on page such and such was metaphorical infanticide. I love literary dinner conversation, especially of the passionate kind. "It's a metaphor, an act of language," yelled Larry, tugging on his omnipresent cap lest he blow his wig. "I don't care about all such as that," Eleanor hollered, hiking up her gown to climb onto the table to come at him to make her point. "He burned up that baby." I thoroughly enjoyed the meal and the passion. And I'm thoroughly in Eleanor's camp if I understand her right. Words are to be taken seriously. I try to take seriously acts of language. Words set things in motion. I've seen them doing it. Words set up atmospheres, electrical fields, charges. I've felt them doing it. Words conjure. I try not to be careless about what I utter, write, sing. I'm careful about what I give voice to. To drive Virginia nuts or Graham to death is not a message I want to send to my heart, my lungs, my brain. My daughter. My readers. Or, to the Grahams and Virginias. But then I come from a particular tradition. I identify with the championship tradition.

Ali, in his autobiography, *I Am the Greatest,* defines a champion as one who takes the telling blow on the chin and hits the canvas hard, can't possibly rally, arms shot, energy spent, the very weight of the body too heavy a burden for the legs to raise, can't possibly get up. So you do. And you keep getting up. *The Awakening* by Kate Chopin is not my classic. *Their Eyes Were Watching God* by Zora Neale Hurston is. Sylvia Plath and the other obligatory writers on women's studies list—the writers who hawk despair, insanity, alienation, suicide, all in the name of protesting woman's oppression, are not my mentors. I was rasied on stories of Harriet Tubman, Ida B. Wells, Paul Robeson, and my grandmother, Annie, whom folks in Atlanta still remember as an early Rosa Parks. So Virginia does not go batty and Graham does not die. Were I to do them in, my granny would no doubt visit me in the night to batter me gingerly about the head and shoulders with an ancestral bone pulled out of the Ethiopic Ocean called the Atlantic.

In the title story of *Seabirds*, I once again focus on resistance rather than despair and dramatize too, I think, the power of words, of utterances. The story is set in Southeast Asia aboard a boat transporting various people with various agenda to the city where the liberation forces, the royalist troops, and the foreign imperialists battle. The central characters are a little girl and her mother. Both are combatants. Both have been tortured. Both resist. When the mother closes her eyes and shivers, the girl fears she is remembering her torture and will begin to chant the words that enable her to come through her ordeal: "Nothing, I'll tell you nothing. You'll never break our spirits. We cannot be defeated." I weave the chant into a flashback scene in which her mother, reliving the experience, thrashes about on the floor while the girl attempts to work a bit of wood between her teeth. I weave it again into the current scene:

> The little girl continued brushing and smoothing her mother's hair, wondering if the gentleman in shoes could be relied upon if her mother bolted. If she herself didn't panic, she would demand he jump to aid the minute the first words were blurted out. "Nothing, I'll tell you nothing." It would take nimble timing, for often the upper folks would not touch the miserable shoeless. "You'll never break our spirits." But then the engine was shut off and her mother relaxed, looking over the side, her face full in the wind. "We cannot be defeated." So. It had been the vibrations of the boat, the little girl concluded, that had made her mother shiver. It had been the lurching of rough waters that had tipped the gentleman away from them.

I am currently working on a novel, though my druthers as writer, reader, and teacher is the short story. The short story makes a modest appeal for attention, slips up on your blind side and wrassles you to the mat before you know what's grabbed you. That appeals to my temperament. But of course it is not too shrewd to be exclusively a short story writer when the publishing industry, book reviewers, critics, and teachers of literature are all geared up for the novel. I gave myself an assignment based on an observation: there is a split between the spiritual, psychic, and political forces in my community. Not since the maroon experience of Toussaint's era have psychic technicians and spiritual folk (medicine people) and guerrillas (warriors) merged. It is a wasteful and dangerous split. The novel grew out of my attempt to fuse the seemingly separate frames of reference of the camps; it grew out of an interest in identifying bridges; it grew out of a compulsion to understand how the energies of this period will manifest themselves in the next decade.

I have three working titles to help me stay focused. "In the Last Quarter" is to remind myself of the period I'm "reading," to remind myself to script flashforwards as well as flashbacks, to remind myself that powerful events of the 1980s and 1990s (nuclear explosions, comet splashdowns, asteroid collisions) resonate in the present. Legionnaire's Disease, for example, may well be a backwash reverberation of the 1984 epidemics that many have predicted. The second title, "The Seven Sisters" (calling all numerologists, astrologers, astronomers, voodooists), helps me to stay within the law of As Above, So Below. In this case I'm trying to link the double helix of the Pleiades constellations (duplicated in the DNA molecule) with one of the central characters—a swamphag healer—and with a traveling troupe of seven women known as sisters of the yam, sisters of the plantain, sisters of the rice, sisters of the corn. These women from the ancient mother cultures perform multimedia shows at rallies and conferences and help me to argue the bridging of several camps: artists and activists, materialists and spiritualists, old and young, and of course the communities of color. The third working reminder is "The

What It Is I Think I'm Doing Anyhow   165

Salt Eaters." Salt is a partial antidote for snakebite. Bleeding the wound and applying the tourniquet, one also eats salt and applies a salt poultice to the wound. To struggle, to develop, one needs to master ways to neutralize poisons. "Salt" also keeps the parable of Lot's Wife to the fore. Without a belief in the capacity for transformation, one can become ossified. And what can we do with a saltlick in the middle of the projects, no cows there?

I'd never fully appreciated before the concern so many people express over women writers' work habits—how do you juggle the demands of motherhood, etc.? Do you find that friends, especially intimates, resent your need for privacy, etc.? Is it possible to wrench yourself away from active involvement for the lonely business of writing? Writing had never been so central an activity in my life before. Besides, a short story is fairly portable. I could narrate the basic outline while driving to the farmer's market, work out the dialogue while waiting for the airlines to answer the phone, draft a rough sketch of the central scene while overseeing my daughter's carrot cake, write the first version in the middle of the night, edit while the laundry takes a spin, and make copies while running off some rally flyers. But the novel has taken me out of action for frequent and lengthy periods. Other than readings and an occasional lecture, I seem unfit for any other kind of work. I cannot knock out a terse and pithy office memo any more. And my relationships, I'm sure, have suffered because I am so distracted, preoccupied, and distant. The short story is a piece of work. The novel is a way of life.

When I replay the tapes on file in my head, tapes of speeches I've given at writing conferences over the years, I invariably hear myself saying—"A writer, like any other cultural worker, like any other member of the community, ought to try to put her/his skills in the service of the community." Some years ago when I returned south, my picture in the paper prompted several neighbors to come visit. "You a writer? What all you write?" Before I could begin the catalogue, one old gent interrrupted with—"Ya know Miz Mary down the block? She need a writer to help her send off a letter to her grandson overseas." So I began a career as the neighborhood scribe—letters to relatives, snarling letters to the traffic chief about the promised stop sign, nasty letters to the utilities, angry letters to the principal about that confederate flag hanging in front of the school, contracts to transfer a truck from seller to buyer etc. While my efforts have been graciously appreciated in the form of sweet potato dumplings, herb teas, hair braiding, and the like, there is still much room for improvement—"For a writer, honey, you've got a mighty bad hand. Didn't they teach penmanship at that college?" Another example, I guess, of words setting things in motion. What goes around, comes around, as the elders say.

It will be a pleasure to get back to the shorts; they allow me to share. I much prefer to haul around story collections to prisons, schools, senior citizen centers, and rallies and then select from the "menu" something that suits the moment and is all of a piece. But the novel's pull is powerful. And since the breakthrough achieved in the sixties by the Neo-Black Arts Movement, the possibilities are stunning. Characters that have been waiting in the wings for generations, characters that did not fit into the roster of stereotypes, can now be brought down center stage. Now that I/we have located our audience, we are free to explore the limits of language. Now that American history, American literature, the American experience is being redefined by so many communities, the genre too will undergo changes. So I came to the novel with a sense that everything is possible. And I'm attempting to blueprint for myself the merger of these two camps: the political and the spiritual. The possibilities of healing that split are exciting. The implications of actually yoking those energies and of fusing that power quite take my breath away.

ERICA JONG

Blood and Guts:
The Tricky Problem of Being
a Woman Writer in
the Late Twentieth Century

The question of whether or not writers are affected by the politics of the times in which they live has always been a tricky one. Some part of them assuredly is—but whether it is the part that tunes into the communal unconscious and makes poems and novels is doubtful. Yet a writer is a person of his or her age and must live in it. For women writers the systematic discouragement even to *attempt* to become writers has been so constant and pervasive a force that we cannot consider their literary productions without somehow assessing the effects of that barrage of discouragement. Often discouraged in the home, often at school, often by families and spouses, the rare woman writer who does not lose her determination along the way is already a survivor. That one should next have to face the systematic discouragement of a male-oriented literary establishment is absurd and sad but nonetheless a real fact of life for many women writers.* The truth is that many of us are doomed to do our best work in an atmosphere of condescension and loneliness. Yet perhaps there is some sense in which that lack of establishment approval is a blessing, for an artist must learn (the sooner the better) that he or she works for the work itself, not for approval, and it is easier to establish that sense of creative independence when approval is lacking than when one is seduced by it. Prizes, awards, rave reviews are, after all, snares, and perhaps they are more destructive to one's sense of creative independence than the systematic discouragement the perpetual outsider receives. Still, we cannot truly understand the situation of the woman writer unless we are honest about this systematic discouragement, and unless we try to see clearly the form it takes, and the strategies of survival it imposes upon the individual artist. School is as good a place to start as any, for school is a microcosm of our society's values.

One of the most notable (and faintly horrifying) memories from my college years is the time a Distinguished Critic came to my creative writing class and delivered himself of the following thundering judgment: "Women can't be writers. They don't know blood and guts, and puking in the streets, and fucking whores, and swaggering through Pigalle at 5 A.M. . . . ." But the most amazing thing was the *response*—or lack of it. It was 1961 or '62, and we all sat there—aspiring women writers that we were—and listened to this Maileresque claptrap without a word of protest. Our hands folded on our laps, our eyes modestly downcast, our hearts cast even lower

* No one has chronicled this repression better than Tillie Olsen in her splendid book *Silences* (1978).

than our eyes, we listened meekly—while the male voice of authority told us what women could or couldn't write.

Things have changed since then. When I went to college (from 1959 to 1963), there were no women's studies courses, no anthologies that stressed a female heritage, no public women's movement. Poetry meant Yeats, Lowell, James Dickey. Without even realizing it, I assumed that the voice of the poet had to be male. Not that I didn't get a good literary education. I did. Barnard was a miraculous place where they actually gave you a degree for losing yourself in a library with volumes of Byron and Keats, Shakespeare and Chaucer, but the whole female side of the library heritage was something I would have to discover for myself years later, propelled by the steam generated by the women's movement.

No Distinguished Critic would dare say such things to a college class today (however much he might think them). Sexism is somewhat better hidden now—though it is far from eradicated. And no college class would sit meekly listening to such rubbish. That is one of the things that has happened in the years since I graduated from college, and I am proud to have been part of the process. Now, when I go to read my work at colleges, I find the students reading and discussing contemporary writing by women as if there never had been a time when a Distinguished Critic could say "Women can't be writers"—even in jest. I am grateful and glad for that change, but it has not been won without pain. Nor is it necessarily a lasting change. Like the feminists of the twenties, we could easily see the interest in female accomplishments once again eclipsed by reactionary sexism, only to have to be passionately rediscovered yet again, several decades later.

It's ironic that Mr. Distinguished Critic should have identified Blood and Guts as the thing that women writers supposedly lacked,* because in the first years of the women's movement, there was so *much* Blood and Guts in women's writing that one wondered if women writers ever did anything but menstruate and rage. Released from the prison of propriety, blessedly released from having to pretend meekness, gratefully in touch with our own cleansing anger, we raged and mocked and menstruated through whole volumes of prose and poetry. This was fine for writers who had a saving sense of irony, but in many cases the rage tended to eclipse the writing. Also, as years went by, literary feminism tended to ossify into convention. Rage became almost as compulsory to the generation of writers who came of age in the late sixties and early seventies as niceness and meekness had been to an earlier generation. Feminists proved that they could be as rigidly dogmatic as any other group. They did not hesitate to criticize works of art on political grounds and to reject poems and novels for dealing with supposedly counterrevolutionary subjects.

This was unfortunate. It was also, I suppose inevitable. Anger against patriarchal stifling of talent had been so pro-

* This is indeed a curious metaphor for what women writers supposedly lack, since of course it is obvious that women are the sex most in tune with the entrails of life, as it were. But we can understand the great critic's condemnation better if we remember that in the nineteenth century women writers were denigrated for their delicacy, their excessive propriety (which supposedly precluded greatness), while in the past decade or so they have been condemned by male critics for their *im*propriety—which also supposedly precludes greatness. The whole issue is a red herring. Whatever women writers do or do not do precludes greatness (in the mind of the chauvinist) simply because they are women. We must see this sort of reasoning for what it is: namely, misogyny. See Mary Ellmann's wonderful book, *Thinking about Women* (1968) on the subjects of sexual stereotypes and phallic criticism. She exposes the hypocrisies of phallic criticism with great wit.

scribed for so many centuries that in letting it loose, many women completely lost their sense of humor. Nor could anyone maintain that getting in touch with anger was unimportant. It was, in fact, a vitally important phase for women's writing to go through. Nothing is more destructive of the spirit and ultimately of creativity than false meekness, anger that does not know its own name. And nothing is more freeing for a woman (or for a woman writer) than giving up the pleasures of masochism and beginning to fight. But we must always remember that fighting is only a first step. As Virginia Woolf points out in *A Room of One's Own,* many women's books have been destroyed by the rage and bitterness at their own centers. Rage opens the doors into the spirit, but then the spirit must be nurtureed. This is hardly easy because women writers (like women) tend to be damned no matter what they do. If we are sweet and tender, we are damned for not being "powerful" enough (not having "blood and guts"), and if we rage, we are said to be "castrating," Amazonian, lacking in tenderness. It is a real dilemma. What is the authentic voice of the woman writer? Does anyone *know?* Does anyone know what the authentic voice of woman is? Is it sweet and low like the voice of Shakespeare's Cordelia, or is it raging and powerful like the voice of Lady Macbeth? Is it an alternation of the two?

The problem is, I suppose, that women have never been left alone to *be* themselves and to find out for themselves. Men need them so badly and are so terrified of losing them that they have used their power to imprison them. To imprison them in castles of stone as long as that was possible, and to imprison them in castles of myth thereafter. The myths were mostly ways of keeping us out of touch with our own strength, and this confused many generations of women. We were told we were weak, yet as we grew older, we increasingly sensed we were strong. We were told that men loved us for our dependency, yet as we grew older, we observed that, despite themselves, they loved us for our independence, and if they didn't—we didn't always care! We found that we could grow only by loving ourselves a little, and loving our strengths, and so, paradoxically, we found we could only grow up by doing the opposite of all the things our culture told us to do. We were told our charm lay in weakness; yet in order to survive, we had to be strong. We were told we were by nature indecisive; and yet, having been told that, our very existence often seemed to depend on our decisiveness. We were told that certain mythic definitions of women were immutable natural laws, biological "facts"; yet so often our very endurance depended upon changing those supposedly unchangeable things, and upon embracing a life credo of change.

In fact, when I look back on the years since I left college, and I try to sum up what I have learned, it is precisely that: not to fear change, not to expect my life to be immutable. All the good things that have happened to me in the last several years have come, without exception, from a willingness to change, to risk the unknown, to do the very things I feared the most. Every poem, every page of fiction I have written, has been written with anxiety, occasionally panic, always uncertainty about its reception. Every life decision I have made— from changing jobs, to changing partners, to changing homes—has been taken with trepidation. I have not ceased being fearful, but I have ceased to let fear control me. I have accepted fear as a part of life, specifically the fear of change, the fear of the unknown, and I have gone ahead despite the pounding in the heart that says: turn back, turn back, you'll die if you venture too far.

I regard myself as a fairly typical member of the female sex, and as a fairly typical member of the class of '63. I may have a greater talent for self-expression, but in my fears and feelings, I am the same. My talent to write may propel me into places and situations I wouldn't otherwise find myself in, but in the dark of night, having insomnia, I think the same thoughts as you or you. I get impatient with successful women who feel that their success has lifted them out of the ordinary stream of women's lives and who say to their fearful, unfledged sisters: I did it against the odds; you can, too. As a writer, I feel that the very source of my inspiration lies in my never forgetting how much I have in common with other women, how many ways in which we are all—successful or not— similarly shackled. I do not write about superwomen who have transcended all conflict; I write about women who are torn, as most of us are torn, between the past and the future, between our mothers' frustrations and the extravagant hopes we have for our daughters. I do not know what a writer would write about if all her characters were superwomen, cleansed of conflict. Conflict is the soul of literature.

I know I would not mind envisioning a world in which my daughter were free *not* to be a feminist,* were free (if she chose to be a writer) not to write about women's conflicts, not to assume that the accident of her gender compelled her work to have a specific creative bias. But I would also like to see a world in which male writers wrote without masculinist bias, in which for example Hemingway's masculinist mythology (and that of many other contemporary American male writers) was perceived as quite as bizarre and hysterical as the most ab-

* I assume here that feminism is necessitated by our patriarchal culture. In a truly egalitarian culture, feminism would be obsolete. Let us all pray for such obsolescence.

surd excesses of militant feminist fiction, and in which consciousness had become so truly androgynous that the adjective itself would be puzzlingly obsolete. Alas, I do not think our culture is heading in this direction. I think, rather, that after a brief flirtation with sensitivity to patriarchal attitudes (brought about by what has been termed the "second wave" of the women's movement—roughly that fleeting half-decade from 1969 to 1974) the culture is sliding back into its habitual sexism (with perhaps a few new wrinkles of equality, created more by the birth-control revolution and the ravages of inflation upon the average family income than by feminist theory). Radical feminists have, in a sense, abetted this process of backsliding by becoming quite as simple-mindedly dogmatic as the most dogmatic male chauvinists, by disassociating themselves from the realities of most women's lives: i.e., a desire for children and warm affective relationships with men. It is unrealistic to assume that after living in families and tribes for millions of years of human evolution, women will suddenly cease to need affective relationships with men and children and become either solitaries or feminist communards. The human need for companionship and sexuality is far stronger than any intellectual theory, and the point is not to keep women from establishing families (a desire that may even be instinctual) but rather to make their *position* in families less that of semislaves and more that of autonomous individuals within the protection of the group.

Where does all this leave the woman writer of our age? Usually in a quandary. As a sharp observer of her society she cannot fail to see that it discriminates against women (often in emotionally crippling and physically murderous ways), but as an artist she cannot allow her vision to be polluted by the ephemeral dogmas of political movements. It is simply not

possible to write a good book that "proves" the essential righteousness of either lesbianism or heterosexuality, childbearing
or its avoidance, man-loving or man-hating. Righteousness
has, in fact, no place in literature. Of course the keen observer
of her culture will feel deeply about the oppression she sees
around her, the inhumanity of man to man, of man to woman,
but her vision of it must be essentially personal, not abstractly
political. Books are not written by committees—at least not
good books. And the woman writer has as much right as any
other artist to an essentially individual and idiosyncratic vision. If we judge her books according to their political "cor-
rectness," we are doing her as great a disservice as if we judged
them according to her looks or her behavior in the voting
booth. Certainly human history is full of such judg-
mentalism—most of it not coming from women—but always
it is antithetical to the creation of works of art.

After saying all of this, I must also gratefully acknowledge
that the second wave of the feminist movement liberated my
writing and was a liberating influence upon my whole life.
How? Not by supplying me with dogma, but by making it
easier for me to look into myself and assume that what I felt as
a woman was also shared by other women (and men). For one
of the most positive by-products of the so-called second wave
of the feminist movement was its discovery of a new audience
of readers—readers both female and male—who came to realize that literary history as we previously knew it was the history of the literature of the white, the affluent, the male, and
that the female side of experience had been almost completely
omitted (except as seen through the eyes of the traditional victors in the war between the sexes *—men). And this audience

* The question of whether or not men are really victors in the war between the sexes is older than Aristophanes' *Lysistrata*. In terms of the dis-

was suddenly passionately interested in dispatches from the center of the female heart which represented a sort of dark continent, a *terra incognita,* the exploration of which was necessary to a full understanding of human consciousness in all its permutations.

From the courage the women's movement gave and from the reinforcement I received from grateful and passionate readers, I learned the daring to assume that my thoughts, nightmares, and daydreams were the same as my readers'. I discovered that whenever I wrote about a fantasy I thought was wholly private, bizarre, kinky—(the fantasy of the Zipless Fuck in *Fear of Flying* is perhaps the best example of this)—I invariably discovered that thousands of other people had experienced the same private, bizarre, and kinky fantasy.

In the past several years, I have learned, in short, to trust myself. Not to eradicate fear but to go on in spite of fear. Not to become insensitive to distinguished critics but to follow my own writer's instinct despite what they say women should or should not write. My job is not to paralyze myself by anticipating judgment but to do the best I can and let the judgment fall where it may. The difference between the woman who is writing this essay and the girl sitting in that creative writing class in 1961 is mostly a matter of nerve and daring—the nerve to trust my own instincts and the daring to be a fool. No one ever found wisdom without also being a fool. Writers, alas, have to be fools in public, while the rest of the human

tribution of society's material goodies and power, they are clearly victors, but there is much reason to believe that their very status as victors has robbed them emotionally—and robbed them of the sort of flexibility and emotional openness women more usually possess. Still, this is the price they pay for their own dominance, and the fact that the underdog has certain emotional advantages should never obscure the fact that she *is* the underdog.

race can cover its tracks. But it is also painfully true that no one avoids being a fool without also avoiding growth, and growth does not, alas, stop with the current feminist vision of reality. It goes on far beyond it.

It seems to me that having now created an entire literature of female rage, an entire literature of female introspection, women writers are ready to enter the next phase—the phase of empathy. Without forgetting how hard-won our rage was, without forgetting how many puritanical voices would still like to censor our sexuality, I think we must consider ourselves free to explore the whole world of feeling in our writings—and not to be trapped forever in the phase of discovering buried anger. The anger has been discovered, unearthed, anatomized, and catalogued. It may be a strong propellant to the creation of literature, but it is hardly the only propellant. Stronger even than anger is curiosity—emotional and intellectual curiosity— the vehicles through which we enter into other states of being, other lives, other historical periods, other galaxies. Patriarchy will have truly crippled women if it prevents us from experiencing our native human curiosity (because that curiosity has been so overlaid with rage at our position in society). The time has come to let go of that rage; the time has come to realize that curiosity is braver than rage, that exploration is a nobler calling than war. As artists, the unknown beckons to us, singing its siren song and making our hearts pound with fear and desire. Let us not tie ourselves to the mast of anger but sail into the unknown, fearful of the future, yet not paralyzed into immobility by fear; *feeling* the fear, yet not letting the fear control us. This is the ultimate test of our blood and guts. Those who pass it will discover new worlds and create a new literature by women truly worthy of our courage, our imagination, and our craft.

MAXINE HONG KINGSTON

The Coming Book

When a worker who knows how much more labor has to be done in no time nevertheless sits idle because caught in a situation where she can't work—visiting in a strange house overnight or eyes closed in the dentist's chair or darkness suddenly fallen deep in the woods—then the visions come assailing.

Once at the dentist's, I shut my eyes and saw The Book—a volume as thick as Joyce's *Ulysses* but not *Ulysses*—fly at me and fly past. Just before its appearance, I heard words from Joyce like music; not having read Joyce for years, I was surprised at the independence of memory. His words reeled out in entrancing rhythms flowing in small and large figure eights looping into infinity without periods and commas. The Joyce ended on the last Yes, and I heard No, no, no, no, and again

No. I almost jumped out of the chair with elation. The universe had doubled! No, more than doubled; it was multiplying by millions. Joyce's day was but one day in a few people's lives, and there are millions of days more, millions of people more. A book of No would balance out a book of Yes, not cynically or unhappily but like a facing page. The Book had flown out of the distance and zoomed past my head.

I felt tired ahead of time for the work to be done to build The Book word by word. If I could finish it, I would never have to write again; in it would be the last word. So far we have only written approximations.

The Book begins with the sound of a telephone ringing, ringing, ringing. Also a radio is playing a rock song, hard electric rock words, which I've forgotten. If I write The Book, I'll have to invent that song.

That's all I glimpsed when The Book zipped by. I will have to make trails of words into that room to find out who answers the phone, who is calling, and what they talk about.

Right now I don't know who these people are or what the room looks like or what city it's in. But it is not me on the telephone, and not me who lives in that room. I wouldn't play a rock station that loud. So, with The Book, I will make a break from the "I" stories I have been writing.

"The telephone rang too loud again and again and again, crashed into the rock music, the top song on the top ten, at inflexible intervals. It was a warm afternoon. . . ." There will next be a rushing about, turning down the radio, grabbing the phone before it stops ringing.

I can't follow this story any further. First I have to finish the stories I couldn't write during childhood because of the years it took to acquire vocabulary.

The Book's pace will be normal, no skips but one moment

moving to the next like the phone's rings. No elisions like "As the years passed. . . ." I heard each full ring and the time before them. And each word of the song. The characters will rush about, but the narration will be deliberate—*ring . . . ring . . . ring.*

I did not *see* the radio or the telephone; The Book begins with two sounds, which are not proper "visions." But I am not an audile, and I believe that if I lose my sight, I will no longer be able to write. I like to look at poetry on the page, the spacing of the lines, the letters. I like rearranging by eye. Blindly composing by voice would bypass reason, miss precision. Both the sounds are modern sounds, technological noises, not the birds and rivers and winds that I like. Harsh rings. Harsh music. Not the epic symphonies that I hear (but can't remember because I don't know notation).

The second paragraph will begin the dialogue. The Book will be filled with voices as heard through machines. When read aloud, it will sound like the Twentieth Century. The reader will not need a visual imagination, only ears.

I heard somewhere that aural hallucinations are a more severe symptom of psychosis than visual ones. But in healthy people, auricular images may be only a more advanced form of imagination than pictures. (I also habitually hear what other people don't hear—firecrackers or gunshots, which may be Chinese music.) The Book will not be a collection of nonsense sounds but English words, a translation of music.

I told a woman who plays viola in a symphony orchestra how uncapturable music is, how I cannot think of organizing the music I hear, but only be its audience. But she said that writing is the most abstract form; the other forms have concomitant human sense organs; music has the ear, and painting the eye, sculpture the hands, and acting and dancing the voice and body. But writing, she said, does not have its organ. She began to cry; I'm not sure why.

I can feel the texture of The Book; it will be modern like science fiction, like black vinyl. The characters will not worry so much about food as they do in my present writings; they can afford phones and a sound system.

When alone, I am not aware of my race or my sex, both in need of social contexts for definition. Visions (and "aurisons"? "audisions"?) come to a human being alone; they are embarrassed away when people watch you humming to yourself or staring at nothing. Yet visions probably don't come from nowhere but grow from what we see everyday and live everyday, which is America. In America, Everyman—the universal human being—is white. (I have been watching a lot of television.) The Book may exclude me as first-person narrator, and the Chinese-American heroines who have interested me may disappear.

"Hello."

"Hello, is it you?"

"Yes. I mean No. Who is this?"

"It's me."

"Oh, it's you. What are you doing?"

"Nothing much. What about you?"

If The Book is an archetype, I needn't be the one to write it. Someone else can write what happens next, and I'd be happy to read it. You can have the opening if you want; it may save you a few moment's work.

You'd save me the time to examine some other sightings, like the town I saw when I got lost in the woods. Also, there were people calling, "We hear you. We're coming. This way. This way." The shingled roofs and white walls and windows turned out to be optical illusions made by the spaces between the leaves and the shaking leaves catching the sun. "This may be how I'll go," I said aloud. "I'll die of starvation and exposure lost in the mountains." When I'd circled the same landmarks twice, I sat on the ground and waited to get some ultimate message while facing death. The leaves and the insects kept on shimmering. Apparently you have no choice about what shows itself. What I did learn was: Don't trust deer trails; they meander and fade. Head downhill, where you'll come to a stream; follow it to town.

JANET BURROWAY

Opening Nights:
The Opening Days

Janet Burroway kept this journal during the first weeks of
writing a novel, *Opening Nights*.

22 June 1978

It seems as if I have been stripping everything carefully away
for several weeks to clear my self for the *ceremonial* undertaking
of the commitment. Got rid of classes, turned down student
summer projects, wrote overdue letters, called the producer
and told him not, after all, to consider casting me as Lady
Bracknell in the Tallahassee summer production (it might
have been good for the novel, to be back in a theatrical setting,
but would also likely have involved that part of the ego's
energy that needs saving most); entered into a no-appoint-
ments frame of mind that has even made me unwilling to say
I'd appear at the beach or the dock at a given hour.

But after three days at work on *The Opening* I am dissatisfied and fretful, driven back as so many times before to keeping a journal. Beginning *The Buzzards* was like this, the first few pages mere rubble of the holy city in my mind.

The attraction of keeping a journal is the possibility of being able to *jot*. (Interesting, in that regard, that I have xxxed and revised that sentence.) The grind, the shit, of fiction, is the need to shape and construct. Letters flow from me. I always intend to let a novel do the same; every time I promise myself that I'll do a quick imperfect draft. (Gabriel shocked me by saying that a first draft could be written in thirty days, 10 pages a day, then revised twenty times). But I can't do so. These three days have yielded six pages, plus an opening about opening *The Opening* that I scrapped entirely. And that are imperfect by a long shot yet. Decisions have to be made in them, about character, the focus of the reader's anticipation, tone— that make it impossible to proceed until the decisions are made.

The image I have of the opening is of Shaara digging a dog's grave in early-morning mist and red Georgia clay. This image has nothing whatever to do with the plot (but is the fifth of my six novels to open with a death—why? Something about beginnings and endings, life cycle?)—the burial of this dog has nothing to do with the plot, or Shaara particularly, and all the significant stuff has to come in sideways. In a way the necessity of the image is that it does make the information come in sideways. *In media res,* more than that, oblique. Can't hop into it: Shaara doesn't want to work with her former husband but does want to meet his wife, about whom she fantasizes. Should I be more direct? Don't think so. Ciardi: literature is never only about ideas but about the experience of ideas. And experience *is* sideways, isn't it? She thinks she is handling the burying of the dog very well. And she is. Only it will haunt her among the later deaths. Maybe this means that it does have to do with the plot in ways that I feel but don't yet see; maybe that is why these last fidgety weeks I have never seriously questioned that it should begin there in the grave. Or maybe it's this: the setting is a theater, and this theater is subprofessional in the boring little town of Hubbard, Georgia, distinctly devoid of glamour. All the same something sinister can surface, and the grave helps establish that, the Georgia earth, the rotting fecundity.

Still at this point, with Shaara thigh-deep in the clay, her son Kevin still asleep in the room with the iguana cage, I have not really decided whether she lost a daughter five years before. A real plot decision, which I can't yet make.

23 June / 2:30 A.M.

Middle of the night gifts:

Shaara operates on pain; Boyd on fear; Nancy on anger.

Shaara is standing in an open grave, Boyd is opening his suitcase, Nancy is opening a letter from Shaara—when we meet each of them.

At the end, Shaara confronts her pain through contact with Nancy; Boyd faces his fear in the burial of the leading lady, Gunilla; Nancy expresses her anger with flight. A letter, a grave, a suitcase. This very schematic thing must be well hidden but here.

Lying there worrying about not wanting it to be a revenge novel against Boyd, which it so much is if Shaara remarries and Nancy leaves him. But the answer to this is Boyd's plight that he operates on fear; it is such a goddamn unacceptable thing for him to do that all his behavior is arranged to hide it from the two women. What a plight for him! Everything we know of him in private reveals it, and the reason he's such a good director is precisely because he draws on his own troubled psyche, his dreams, when he works with actors. Yet everything that he says/does to the two women is designed to conceal his terror from them, so they *do* totally misunderstand him, take it out on him; nobody's fault.

I had already known that Boyd's fear was *my* point of contact with him, how I get into his skin: terror at facing the actors, terror of the telephone, which comes out in clipped competence, sometimes brilliance, sometimes brutality.

Yeah, yeah. Freen came home very late from work tonight, asked how it was going. Told him over midnight tuna fish that the angst of right now is having written enough to have spoiled the amorphous luminous Whole Idea of it that exists in the mind before you start, but not enough to have got hold of the specific thing it will be, who they are, what will happen. When I say this sort of thing, Freen nods, waits, watches, smiles. My husband knows me well enough to know that what I need is neither cheer nor advice, but a willing audience.

This feels like getting nearer. Like y'know, plot. At the end Nancy operates on her anger, Shaara faces the stunting pain and operates against it by marrying Josh. Boyd? Is undone by the fear? Or no: the worst thing that can happen to him happens. The star *dies:* the show does not go on. And it isn't that terrible. It can be survived. Somebody offers him a job out of it. What a goddam fuckin' happy ending.

If I had not gone through this dreary week, a week earlier than my schedule called for; if I had not decided that, once for all, I do not like to write and like it less and less, that neither writing nor reading even the greatest books constitutes a purpose for me and therefore the whole enterprise is not worth undertaking; if I had not, as I keep advising my students, chained myself to my chair, then I would not be sitting here postcoital, urgent, and "inspired" at three A.M., happy. There are more bad hours than good on a novel (a marriage, a parenthood, a life?) but I knew that at 19 fahchrissake and have relearned it hourly-yearly since; if you don't put in the bad ones you don't earn the good. Calvin taught me that?

Also told Freen this:

The novels that I get most lost in, can't put down, tend the last few years to be by women: Godwin, Drabble, Lurie, Gould. I admire Spark, Adler, Lessing, and Didion more, for experimentation, form, the shape of their ideas, but I can be more easily distracted from them. The novels that sorta awe and dazzle me, and which I would like to emulate although I sometimes find them heavy to get through, tend to be by men: Barth, Barthelme, Pynchon, Robbins, and McGuane. I am more in tune with the women's work, but I would like to stretch in the other direction. Don't think this is a simple sexist remnant. (I remember similarly wanting to *read* Trollope but *be* Conrad.) What I dislike about the women's work I like is that within and between and among the understanding, compassion, psychology, forgiveness, is an underlying trivial complaint; a bitch against life. What I love about the men's work is its celebration: love of the Baby Ruth wrapper in the gutter, a celebration of American roadside rubbish. And yet this luv luv luv does seem to me: easy. Super-facial.

What's troubled me about the opening Shaara chapter is that it's got the roadside rubbish (I am conscious of her eating granola crumbs, out of a vendor, on a naugahyde couch) but it doesn't celebrate; it's tired and hurt and mad. But leave that for the present and go on. If it's going to have a happy ending after all maybe it will celebrate in the end.

This reminded me of a picnic at Uncle Walt's and Aunt

Ida's in Riverside California when I was 13. One of those family reunions we used to trek to, leaving Phoenix at three A.M., driving over the desert in the wee hours with our heads wrapped in wet towels, running from the rising sun.

At this one, I remember, I very specifically discovered that I liked men and did not like women. Because the men were in the backyard with us kids, telling anecdotes, especially Uncle Walt, cutting up, being fun. Uncle Walt had, after Aunt Anne left him in such a state by running off with the Philosophy Professor from Whittier, become a real life hero by contracting a middle aged romance with Ida-of-my-mother's-match-making, whole thing so romantic, and here was Ida *bitching* from the kitchen about the table not being set or the chicken carved or some such crap. And I thought of the older generation, Aunt Charlotte with her "poise" in the kitchen, carping to Uncle John at his croquet; it came to me at once and definitively out of the experience of my extended family that I liked men and not women because men were easy-going and women were bitches.

This was based on reunions and picnics.

Why did Aunt Anne run off?

I thought of it later as *I* bitched. The source of the bitching is that women set the table and serve the chicken. Especially at picnics. It is hard, and that's the truth of it, to have an easy-going nature over a hot stove.

Mostly women and children are linked as victims. But in this respect maybe men and children are natural allies, not needing to deal and not wanting to deal and having no respect for the dealing with the daily nittygrit. The one thing I most resent in my children is the one thing I have most resented in men: insufficient attention to, insufficient appreciation of, the massive organization of mundane detail.

Thas what a novel is, ain't it?

Maybe a journal's a good idea if I can not reread it. Much of this preceding can go into the book for Nancy. She would remember such a picnic and realization. When Boyd goes away on the road the first thing she does is let the dishes sit. (Whereas Shaara, before a job, dusts Kevin's room; her basic impulse is domestic organization.)

24 June

Paradox surfaces at dinner. That my boys are radically unlike each other is no news, but it takes a new shape. Tim's in favor of capital punishment, admires the word *conservative,* thinks "as long as we were in Vietnam we should have gone all out to win." I would think these views natural to the age of fourteen if he had not always been conservative, preferred the most disciplined of his teachers, shown extreme modesty from the age of six. Alex at eleven is radical-liberal in all his views, political, sexual, social. At five he defended his right to play house by announcing he was a feminist. Confessed to me last year with real and obvious guilt that the idea of homosexuality "put him off, so far." Yet Tim is personally a peacemaker and Alex an authoritarian. I also, I notice, am a liberal and a troublemaker. And Freen, who has never been known to make an issue where there is none, is the paradigm of the Willing To Let Live, often surprises me by the firmness of his discipline, sometimes makes me uneasy with the brutality of his wit, now amazes me by defending Tim. He has no patience with disruptive activists, will not espouse feminism as a Cause but only, perpetually, in practice.

I'm reminded of a formula I once read, that anger leads to radicalism and fear to conservatism. It occurs to me that there are fewer phonies among conservatives. Conservatism is based

on self-interest: there's no *need* to be insincere. Whereas liberal-
ism rests on a belief in others and brotherhood, a harder stance
to feel, the self-interest involved is likely to be a high opinion
of one's own virtue, so hypocrisy's an inherent danger.

Still thinking of nittygrit and mundane detail, the men I
have known who have known how to share it; am surprised to
discover that three are as close as brother, father, and husband.
(15 years with men who did not has maybe obscured this.)
Over the late news I observe aloud that really Freen is fatal-
istic, disinterested and uninterested in issues, policies and politics. Yes, he says, because "I really live in our daily life." So
do I, of course, and that we concur in this makes our daily life
serene and full of interest, yet I feel the need to search constantly for the cosmic metaphor. "The family is a microcosm of
nations" sort of thing. He feels no such need, and maybe this
is a role-related difference: I must justify my interest in the rec
room by reaching out to Great Events. He has confidence
enough in the significance of the immediate. I often say of my
dad that he has to be a happy man, since his major interest is
daily maintenance; there's so much of it. The same is so of
Freen, though more of his maintenance is emotional.

27 June

A sort of calm has descended after three very bad and muddled
days (is it only two?) and after I have tried to disengage a little
of the muddle here I am going to try to do a *rough,* as fast as
possible, as many pages as possible, of Nancy after Boyd leaves:
phone call to mother, the mess around her, phone call to
the Dr., opening the mails, phone call to Boyd. This outline
sounds dull and if necessary I will write it dull. When I find
the point of interest I will redo it. May some power please keep
me to this plan for this day amen.

This journal has become either valuable or destructive in that I want to do it, think about writing it, possibly because it's easier than the book.

Remembering the journal I kept in Illinois in The Awful Time. I did not yet know if I had the courage to go through with the divorce, most of the time I didn't know if there'd be money enough for hot dogs by Saturday night. I could not get on with *Raw Silk* (still called *Warp,* then, I think.) On the visit (The Awful Visit) back to New York, I spoke to a Harper & Row editor (a very nice woman—I was conscious that I would find her sympathetic if I were not spaced out with terror; the moldy plush Victorian setting in which we met filled me with a sense of decay). She suggested kindly that I should keep, for publication, a day-to-day journal of the separation trauma I was going through. I inferred, despairing, that this psychological record would be more valuable than any literary contribution I might make. And I insist this is a real problem, perhaps moral, certainly literary, certainly psychological. Literature is a making, not an outpouring. I can't teach otherwise than to insist on this continually. And I believe it. "Self-expression" leads too quickly to self-indulgence, writing fiction is the verbal counterpart (perhaps substitute, surrogate, the thing that will do) of self-control, self-determination. Anyway I kept the journal, knowing that I would not allow it to be published (it seemed to me like a perpetual cry, inarticulate and unattractive; Oh! oh! oh! arggh! save me! I can't stand it! on and on); whereas the fact that it had been suggested to me spoiled it as therapy, the kindly stranger over my shoulder seeing to my soft middle. It wasn't good. But I was able to use much of it later, when I was capable of *making* again.

There's a great problem of timing. I work on a life clock that allows me summers and vacations to write; I'm lucky to have it, most people get two weeks off in the summer. But the novel to be written works on a clock of its own, and so does my own psychological state of readiness. It is virtually impossible to get the three together. When by accident I do, the writing is wonderful ("Too Tightly in Warm Hands" written in 36 consecutive hours, the last 125 pages of *Raw Silk* in three weeks)—I meant that it feels wonderful to write but the writing is also the best that I do, at those times. Now I've set up an unusually good year, with summer off, autumn teaching in Florence, a sabbatical in winter, teaching here in spring, summer off: nine out of the next fifteen months to write. *The Opening* has been around my mind for three years (why am I so slow?—I wish I could sit down and turn out a book a year like Murdoch; or, like a person of Victorian self-control, take a brisk walk before breakfast, sit down to do my five pages before lunch, read in the afternoon, dine at 7 etc.). The book is not as ready as I thought it was, not as ready as *Eyes* was when I began; still it is readier than either *Buzzards* or *Raw Silk*. So that, as I chatter to my colleagues, if I don't write it "it will be my fault."

But I am not in the right state of psychological strength. These three days have been as if lifted out of the Illinois awful time and dropped into the stillness and stability around me now. Not quite accurate either. I've been building up for fear. Simply: I've been in touch with madness and suicide for longer than I realized. What the confrontation in Illinois did was to make me aware of it, and the strength that surviving it has given me is negated by the realization, which carries its own fear. This seems as near as I can come to saying it and yet by virtue of its being in words is both melodramatic and a lie. Shit. Of all the human tools invented, who would pick words to work with, the clumsiest for the job at hand? Shovels dig, wheels roll, levers lift, but words do not express.

Dr. Alexander told me that I was not a manic-depressive but a hyperthalamic because I am able to function in both my high and low states. (For someone so angry at words) I take great consolation in a defining term, and this seemed true to me also.

I said to Doug yesterday that I wished for a little of his nature, able simply to go to the office and get on with it, and he said: oh, but not with a novel, not with a novel. I mentioned this to Merri last night and she said nobody dredges up the self-loathing Doug does when working on a novel: we indulged, laughing, in a self-loathing contest and I was a little relieved.

It is a question of self-loathing. Bad days, disfocused, entirely egotistical, guilty at egotism, loathing self for guilt.

Sunday I had a long headache and I cried a lot. Torn between hiding it and revealing it. Hedged on this by announcing it to Freen as tedious. He said: no, it isn't tedious. I said I did not know why. He said: I don't know why you're doing it either. The crux: I am doing it. It feels as if it is being done to me but I am doing it. Dealing, oh so competently, with suicidal students, I have learned to say this.

Sunday I had headaches and cried a lot, scared myself thinking about death, scared myself about wearing out the family's patience, had some bad dreams. That's all. I can give the dream to Nancy even if I cut it out later. And I suppose, again, that's why I write.

But is it by now the process of writing itself that brings the problem it is necessary to write out? Often feels like it. Writing well is a joy but so is making a good dress, and usually when I can write with joy I can also make a good dress.

I do not admire giving up. People who keep demanding attention in the guise of giving up bore and anger me. In *Lovers and Tyrants* du Plessix Gray strikes a strong note, says that what men dislike most in women is what they fear in themselves: hysteria, breakdown, not coping. Struck me at the time that what women dislike in men is also what they fear in themselves: violence, brutality, hatred, contempt. What I love in Freen is what I would like to have in myself: patient stillness. "I have everything I need." His level of expectation for every day is commensurate with the day's rewards. Mine is not.

29 June

I remember that the BBC interviewed E. M. Forster when I was an undergraduate at Cambridge. The interviewer asked him whether he'd found writing easy or hard. I enjoyed it, he said blandly. But when an undergraduate he'd taken to asked him why he never wrote another after *Passage to India,* he said: Oh, it was too hard.

No writing yesterday; went out with a crew from WFSU-TV to be filmed into the settings of a documentary on the Apalachicola River, so that when I do the narration it will appear that the whole thing was my idea and doing. That feeling again that I should have followed my childhood impulse and gone into film, and perhaps I can use this for Boyd Soole—right, in fact. He is discouraged by the legit theater as I am discouraged by the novel, the form in the process of becoming passé. Filming is tedious, long, hard, and hot. We did four locations covering about 200 miles, just under a hundred degrees all the way while I was being taught to drive an outboard motor, then faked being comfortable with it in and out of the cypress swamps, then after a couple of hours was comfortable with it and enjoyed myself a lot. Then climbing down a root path so they could get a zoom shot of the panorama at the bottom of a cliff, hiking back up again sweating to the tips of my hair, fantasies of heart attack, determined cheerfulness. Then an interview with 87-year-old beekeeper Aunt Belle. This was curiously tense because they have really already filmed the interview and I had to make my questions fit into it, though this is not something Aunt Belle would understand, so in effect I had to make not conversation but the *same* conversation without appearing stupid to her. Note of panic when she accused director Melissa of intending to put her "on the TV." But Melissa handled this beautifully, ignored it until we'd all become easy with each other, then Aunt Belle said it again, Melissa said, "Why, Aunt Belle, you know we are!" and laughed. Aunt Belle shrugged, "I don't care what you do." Don't know that I could have handled this so well.

Two things seriously attract me about the process, the most important being the camaraderie. Sticky-hot tedious stuff, but we're in it together and mutually aimed at the beer at the end. Reminded me of costuming, the most humanly fulfilling job I've had, the same tedium and long hours, the same communal assumption that we will keep at it and get it done in time. Writing is *lonely*.

The other thing that seems easier (not necessarily more rewarding, just easier) is that there's so much more real and objective subject matter for it all to be based on. Melissa has got all the muddle of choice of shot, editing 12 hours of film down into a half-hour, a real mess of selection and arrangement. But this film is about the Apalachicola and there it is. She must choose that I narrate, and what I say, and where I stand and walk while my voice is over, but when she has done so the camera hits me, draws back, pans the river, and *there it is*. She doesn't also have to produce and invent the river. Neither it nor I have got to be dug out of mind and gut.

I sit here (also lie awake mornings) in front of decisions to make of an inventive kind, not myself in a decisive frame of mind, and am reminded of standing in front of the meat counter in the supermarket in Mohamet, Illinois, unable to decide what to cook for Gail Godwin for dinner. Unable to choose chicken or beef, to remember what one did with them. *Unable.* Failure of energy and will.

Decisions on the novel this morning: second wife's name is not Nancy but Wendy, much better, though "she had more Peter Pan than Wendy about her, a boneless boyish sexiness." Boyd and Wendy live in New York, she goes to Vermont. But where is her mother? It matters a lot, the "status detail" that Tom Wolfe says is one of the four essentials of fiction (and he's right; clue to Wendy's personality, what she was molded by—all I know for sure is that it was a germ-free childhood, riskless. But what style of germ-free and riskless, Scottsdale or Boston? Gotta get this right today.) Shaara went from Burlington, Iowa, to Hubbard, Georgia, but via where? Has she traveled? Boyd now does the northeast stock circuit and an occasional off-off-Broadway, but where's he from?

Reading Edith Wharton I register again how right Wolfe is too: half the social satire is in the character's judgments on the wine, floral arranging, sauce, carriages, etc. of other characters. Like Wolfe's. If I can make these style decisions about my characters then maybe the literary style will follow without all this self-conscious wrenching.

1 July

I have 21 pages, unusable, unprintable, destructive of the book as my mind still partly sees it, contradictory of character and inconsistent in tone. But I am undoubtedly started. For peace of mind, though I'd prefer to be able to go on, I must go back now and clean them, mold them.

In this beginning state, which feels inert and will-less, relevance is nevertheless everywhere, and that probably means I'm writing. From Rock to Rilke. I turn on the radio: Paul Simon is complaining that he's still crazy too, the Beatles advise letting it be, while the Eagles want me to take it to the limit; and somebody whose name I don't catch promises me she'll sing me *her* song as soon as she finds her voice. I read Rilke:

> . . . if only we arrange our life according to that principle which counsels us that we must always hold to the difficult. . . .

> Should one perhaps seek rescue in some quiet handicraft and not be fearful for whatever fruit may be ripening deep within one, behind all the rouse and stir? . . .

> In writing poetry, one is always aided and even carried away by the rhythm of exterior things, for the lyric cadence is that of nature: of the waters, the wind, the night. But to write rhythmic prose one must go deep into oneself and find the anonymous and multiple rhythm of the blood. Prose needs to be built like a cathedral; there one is truly without a name, without ambition, without help; on scaffoldings, alone with one's consciousness.

This last rings particularly true; a defense, a forgiveness. And yet of course the rhetorical swing is embarrassingly lofty set alongside a little novel that begins, "Shaara Soole was thigh-deep in a red clay Georgia grave at seven A.M. in a May mist." I am not building a cathedral but a Dunkin' Donuts. Under Rilke's angst is a pre-wars assumption that it is ultimately worthwhile to write. In this volatile, weak, irritable (and yes, timid is the right word) frame of mind, I am quite simply ashamed of myself. All those quirks of personality which, after great things have been accomplished, are labeled sensitivity, temperament, anguish of the artist, genius, are only, if you ain't a genius, irritability, hysteria, a bore and burden to your family. I am not treating the family badly, but it's precisely that that is dishonest. Wharton describes May Welland thus: "She was trained to conceal imaginary wounds under a Spartan smile." Instead of that, I would like to be quite open and accurate about why I am sometimes brittle, sometimes inert, sometimes unjust. But it would bore them all the more.

And on the other hand would like to be a true Spartan, not to be concealing imaginary wounds but to imagine no wounds.

Not saying what I mean.

Writing is very like depression (including its lifting, for me, in the evening, so that at the moment I have allowed myself leisure I would, of course, be quite capable of writing a clean crisp scene). The thing about depression is that others can have only so much sympathy for it. B's last two suicide threats left me cold and angry; she had used me up. We now know that Rilke, Woolf, Conrad, Sexton, Plath, suffered greatly over their writing, suffered because they wrote and wrote because they suffered, and we respect it because they did the stuff—and we don't have to live with them. We don't know what Clara Rilke and Leonard Woolf suffered in daily exasperation. We assume with hindsight that it was worth it: was it at the time? What nitpicking mediocre half-assed writers suffer may well be the same, and they don't *save* it. But you never know which you are. You just got no choice. Rhetorically, loftily, Rilke advises the young poet Kappus that if he would die if he couldn't write, then he should write, otherwise not. This seems tinny, a horoscope or a Cosmopolitan questionnaire. As I take the questionnaire I ask myself the question. And I dunno. I would sure like to be relieved of the necessity to write, love the periods when I "seek rescue in some quiet handicraft" and would be relieved to have that permanently the case. But I cannot, in 1978, after a fifties Arizona childhood and with these gawky 21 pages behind me, speak with any conviction of a necessity of the soul.

2 July / 12:20 A.M.

Went to see Polanski's *Tenant* tonight; turned off after ten minutes; pretentious and boring though this is perhaps more my mood than the fault of the film. Much more interested as it went on in pursuing my own line of thought, with relation to Boyd.

Doug Fowler's idea that every author has only one story to tell which he tells over and over (mine is deciding not to give up). *Tenant* is the same film exactly as *Rosemary's Baby:* moving into the empty apartment where someone has died, finding menace in the old wardrobe—a mystery behind it, it has got to be moved—and the nearly normal interference of the neighbors. Produces a hysteria which everybody takes to be insanity; turns out that even those outside the building are in on it, when the protaganist turns to them for help.

Instantly connects with something I already arbitrarily stuck into Boyd's intro:

Gunilla Lind: Do you believe in the occult?

Boyd: Only as a metaphor for the horrors of ordinary life.

This is both me and him, a point of contact, except I admit that I find the horrors of ordinary life the real horrors. He must do otherwise. Hides in the metaphor.

What can be more ordinary than, in Polanski, the menace underneath the neighbors complaining about the noise? Connects also to Shaara and burying of the dog: you take death on, she says. Rage and terror attach themselves to the complaints of neighbors, the screech of tires, dark rooms, musty smells, the simple squeaking of a rusty hinge. The occult is invented as an explanation of our rage and terror, as gods are invented as an explanation of our awe and hope, nobility. Really we do not know why we are terrified, enraged.

Boyd can work this out on theoretical level as I do here as long as the novel does it in experience.

So many modern dramatists center on the room. Pinter where the room is safety and the danger is the opening door. Albee where the room is a trap. Ibsen's Hedda smothered, his Nora constricted in the *Doll's House.* Beckett's *Endgame* where the room is the deranged mind—or is it? Polanski's new tenants where the mundane innocence is destroyed by something present in the place, the walls.

Boyd aware of this but for him the present and personal horror is the stage, the place he has chosen; a space that pretends to be a room but which is in fact exposure. He can dream that the motel room loses its fourth wall and the audience observes him there, where he hides his fear.

The motel menace: he likes its anonymity but it means that his own center must hold; identity is dependent on him. The TV set as a window onto blood and death; he flicks it on, to war, hijacking, mugging, murder; will he always be able to switch it off? Check if *Rosemary's Baby* or *The Tenant* have been on late night TV. These could spark off this train of thought for him as for me.

4 July

Sitting here now (with twenty people due in a couple of hours to celebrate our Independence), trying to mold and make, rewriting and rewriting these first Shaara pages, I'm reminded of the gentle author in Camus' *Plague,* who spent years perfecting the first sentence of his great opus, the message being that he would never write it. The message being that, in writing as in any other endeavor, you must choose compromise, you must forgive yourself and *settle for* if anything is to be accomplished. And yet there's no point in writing adequately. This, above all, is why it's so hard. Everything else that I do I do to fulfill a need, and if some days I teach only adequately, well then, all the same some information passes from me to those who have arrived at the appointed hour asking for information. If I mother only adequately, all the same the children must be fed and bedded. Nobody needs another novel. The only justification for writing one is that it should be *wonderful*. Adequate is inadequate. So I sit and pass judgment on myself: this is dull, this is unclear, this is insignificant: ergo I am dull, I am unclear, I am insignificant.

5 July

Boyd is;
a huge man
perpetually untidy
one of those people who pop a button the first time he puts on a shirt
lumbering in a bear of a body
a boiled man, a failed missionary still sweating from the cannibal's pot
sometimes he dreams that his own body is chasing him
he exudes an abstracted intelligence; people never think he is listening to them and are surprised when he acts on what they've said
he creates a space and a wake with his presence, and this above all is what has made him a successful director
and a successful lover. Men and older, competent women, read only the authority in him and defer to it

young women, beautiful women, sense his vulnerability and
this, the soft core in so large a presence, endears him
he has never had any trouble getting women
between Boyd and Shaara there was too much presence, too
much will, too much flesh
they were both diminished by the confrontation
their energies, maybe weary of collision, left them, and they
dwindled into some such state as may be described by the
word fidget
Wendy Soole like a bright bird perched on his wrist
a songster on a statue

July 6

Tim is packing for Pittsburgh, not this time for a vacation
but, for the first time, for a whole school year with his father.

The dreams and supine obsessions of the bad years, the
ones that persist in memory and still rise off the pages of my
journal with the original pain, have to do with the house in
England. The recurrent dream of its not being mine, of elegant and proper women disbelieving that I was ever mistress of
such a place. If I believe Freud that all dreams are wish-fulfill-
ments (I do not), then this one meant that I wished to be rid of
it, to repudiate the elegance and propriety it signified. I can
see this. But I loved it and can still love its memory.

I never dream of losing this home; there is no reason that I
should. But I sometimes dream that I am still in my first marriage and can convince no one otherwise. Or I dream that my
mother tells me I've made a mistake: the ceremony that took
place six months ago involved someone I vaguely remember
from high school; it is socially embarrassing that I am living
with Freen, and I must hold a *very large* party with the intent
of reassuring everyone that I will move back to Phoenix as soon

as it's practicable. These are the dreams and supine obsessions that I know will persist and in ten years' time rise off the page with the original pain.

Wake in a sweat and know what these dreams have to do with Tim packing: the past is never over; I cannot undo the choices of my younger self.

7 July

Reading *Revelations,* an anthology of women's diaries put together by Mary Jane Moffat and Charlotte Painter, reading it too avidly, partly to avoid writing. I laugh with the pleasure of recognition over Mary Boykin Chestnut:

> I think this journal will be disadvantageous for me, for I spend my time now like a spider spinning my own entrails, instead of reading as my habit was in all spare moments.

And I identify, with immense hope, with George Eliot:

> Few women, I fear, have had such reason as I have to think the long sad years of youth were worth living for the sake of middle age. Our prospects are very bright . . . I am writing my new novel.

I also identify, more grimly, when Käthe Kollwitz speaks of feeling parched, "almost long[ing] for the sorrow again," as if being filled with sorrow were more bearable than emptiness.

And I feel a surprised delight (very little irony in it) that it is Virginia Woolf who provides the most reasonable example of going on with it, however pointless it seems. Writing *The Moths* (later *The Waves*) she began in a disoriented despair, with no "great impulse" or "fever" but with only a "great pressure of difficulty." Five months later she is calm and business-like; the novel, she says, is "trudging along." And five months later still she finishes ecstatic, "reeling," with "moments of such intensity and intoxication that I seemed only to stumble after my own voice." May the Muse grant me such stumbling.

8 July

Sometimes I dream of writing, or rather having written, a novel in great speed, and so automatically that it is a kind of *Kubla Khan.* I do not, in the dream, remember having written it, only it is there, unpolished and imperfect, with the publishers, who turn it down. To remember this dream is like a dream. I have seen *Targets* and *Chinatown* (the latter for the fourth time) tonight, and Freen has gone to Mike and Cindy's to see *Targets* again privately. This is something I don't understand but vaguely respect. It's a bad movie but he wants to know bad movies. It irritates him when A. requires the reading of snippets of minor southern writers, but he wants to learn, study, know, everything there is to know about movies good and bad. Freen will know celluloid like I know nothing on earth with the possible exception of my own mental pattern and process. Anyway. I did not want to see it again so have come to moil over the failure of this opening of *The Opening.* Didn't write today, which was totally absorbed in the failure to clear a drainpipe from the washing machine in order to save the price of a plumber. The difference between this marriage and my first is that it took both our days. That, and that I respect his desire to see a bad film twice. I have no contempt in me for his concerns. I suppose that if I could ask for one good, one lasting good, in life, it would be to maintain and retain this respect for his concerns.

And then this image of the automatic novel as in the dream. That I should scrap *The Opening* and just begin to write what happened on the beach last December and January. Ian, still beautiful and burdened, Bernie the ex-beautiful boy, his gayness and his gaiety, the incredible universal love that makes him transcend whatever he encounters. S. who is trying to try to kill herself and whom Bernie ought above all to understand but does not. K., blond, beautiful, talented, translucent as kodachrome and wasting her life in a pet of misguided love, misvalued values. Freen as still as the beach itself, an unacceptable lover for me by every standard the world provides, and yet in this context, this strange agglomeration, loved by everyone. Why? Because they love me (I would have to be there but I don't see myself) and they see his stillness, patience, as the sand against which I crash and crash, never utterly effacing it. Somehow these friends give me permission to strew my childhood lessons and marry this beach.

In *The Opening* this is what Wendy does for Shaara. But if I had the guts, or rather, if I could write for 700 consecutive hours, this story of the beach is the novel I would write instead.

8 July

A moderate blessing-counting mood. I sit hour after hour, reading snippets of myself and others, not knowing (as Auden accurately observed) whether I am procrastinating or must wait for it to come, but not wanting to avoid the desk. Wanting to be here in fact. And the fact is that I can be. The children are of an age and Freen of a disposition that there is no hour of the day or night I can't say: I want to work, and do so. This is something I have never had before, or when I had to have it, I had to *take* it with great violence. The kids are noisy and negligent, and Freen, I am perfectly certain, is *wrong* about the washing machine! but there is no turmoil under. I forget. M. came into the kitchen on 4th of July with a face blank, numb with suffering over a marital quarrel and I thought: oh, oh, I forgot what it's like. I forgot to bless that base of a life without violence and turmoil, where I may concentrate on the little torture of writing a book.

And some ideas come. Boyd is directing Manet's *The Nuns,* and he will point out to the actors that one theme of it is this: the Mother Superior makes up a horror story to frighten the Senora. And then it comes true. Again and again in *The Opening* this happens, not with horror stories only but with adventure fantasy (Wendy) and romantic fairy tales (Shaara). A good theme for me, one I believe in: "what men dream about they do." In this book everybody's dream comes true, only of course when a dream comes true it no longer has the quality of being a dream. You must live with the consequences. You get to the moon: it's made of earth. The point about Boyd is that he knows all this stuff intellectually, is brilliant about it, and specifically keeps saying it's like real life. Only he never sees that it's like his life, now. Doris Lessing's stunning notion that we are waiting for an apocalypse that we are in fact going through.

Now, here is the connection of all that with the imagery of opening. An earthquake. First there is a tremor. Nothing happens but that a few plates slide off the shelves. Then there is a little crack in the earth; it may close up again. But it doesn't this time. People and houses fall into it, die. The mouth, the vagina, the heart, loosen and begin to open. They can recoil and seal themselves again. But they don't this time. The landscape is utterly altered.

The conversation at the end of the book between Shaara and Wendy must have this form precisely: they open a little to each other, subside, withdraw. A chance remark opens it again. Then there is a dangerous violence of empathy. Neither could say at what moment they begin playing out their fantasies of each other. But all of a sudden they are confessing their fantasies of each other, and after that there's no going back. Each gives the other *permission* for the change each wants in her life, and the landscape is utterly changed.

> Shaara: He's younger than I, small boned. He's uninterested in money and contemptuous of power. He's unsocializable. He's the least appropriate choice of all my inappropriate choices.
>
> Wendy: To whom?

I have the wrong personality for a writer. I am too loquacious, live too much in talk. "Real" writers do not talk about work in progress (and also do not, in the popular stance, know what it "means"). Whereas when I dislike what I have on the page, feedback reassures me that it has potential. Last week Merri sent me back refreshed to work, yesterday Peter. Unable to get it on the page I talked to him, mentioned Boyd's sense that he'd missed his vocation, forest for the trees, because in his childhood obsession with horror flicks it never occured to him that they could be a *profession*, an *art*. He went east and studied Ibsen. Peter said: that happened to me! And it occurred to me for the first time that this is very likely a common chord. Sent me back to work.

10 July

Tim is in Pittsburgh, which turns out to be neither neverneverland nor the moon. He is at a distance of eighty-five cents. His voice cracks over the wire: I've gotta wear *trousers* to this school!

And (predictably) out of the unnecessary grief, the unlooked-for gifts. Boyd's breakthrough is not that he handles the death of Gunilla, which would be a professional triumph, the sort he is used to. It is that he breaks through to his son.

I begin to discover how many of the openings are reopenings, which means digging up the past, grave-robbing, body-snatching.

Wendy has to go home and see her mother to encounter fear; it is the trip she avoids for most of the book.

Shaara has not dealt with the failure of her marriage. Big-boned, redheaded, sentimental, she has plenty of outlets that let her avoid it: she weeps at minor kindnesses and television ads for Save-the-Children. What Josh represents to her is the possibility of trying a family again, and she's too hurt to do it on her own. She says to him (implicitly, maybe in so many words): you can only once have the illusion of permanence. And he says: but a second time you may have the intention of it.

Boyd. Has not faced that his parents' accident on the L.A. Freeway was no accident. His father left no note, because his father would confide in no one. But Boyd found other notes, letters, and knows; fears his own dreams are like his father's, fears his son's dreams are like his own. In the first act of *The Nuns,* the Senora is murdered and buried. In the second act they dig her up again. One night Boyd brings his son Kevin back to Shaara's house, they feel something's wrong, they explore and find that possums have dug up the dead dog. (I knew there was a reason for beginning with that dog.) Check Richard Wilbur's poem on this. Together they deal with it; they even specifically spare Shaara the maggots, the stench, the knowledge that her grave wasn't good enough. In the reburying of the dog Boyd comes to the point of telling Kevin about his own father's suicide, and it is this that makes Boyd not-his-father.

Because of it he can deal with Gunilla's death quite competently, without panic; he has already dealt with the real thing. Even possible that Wendy need not leave him; after he has, emotionally, accomplished this, she may say: I have to do this and that for myself, and he can say: so then.

Out of this also emerges a subsidiary theme to do with professionalism. Wendy is a rank amateur at everything, and succeeds with beginner's luck. Picaresque strength; she so *trusts,* that danger avoids her, and when she confronts it she can say: don't you dare! Whereas Shaara, Gunilla, Boyd are all intensely professional. Because Boyd is, he manipulates Gunilla into the performance he wants from her. Because she is distressed by this she tries to open up to Shaara, who will not: it would be unprofessional to undermine the director. Because she is professional Shaara will not alter the cut of the neckline for the sake of Gunilla's modesty. So Gunilla's breasts fall out in rehearsal when they must lash her "corpse" to the post. Professionally, Boyd does not question Shaara's costume design, but will alter the blocking so that Gunilla is lashed at the neck instead of the ribs. Because she is a professional, Gunilla will not cry out as she chokes. So all are equally responsible for her death.

And out of all *this* tumbles a new title. I had got it wrong. The book is about the opening of a grant-funded summer theater. But the star dies, and the theater does not open. What opens is: Josh and Shaara; Shaara and Wendy, Boyd and Kevin. Sex, friendship, parenthood, love and death, all at night. And the title is not one opening but *Opening Nights.*

11 July

In my procrastination-or-waiting-for-it-to-come yesterday I reread the journal of the awful year Illinois-to-Tallahassee. Peculiar that I look back on terrible times with affection. The Greeks knew the opposite, that "no suffering is greater than remembering happier times."

I see why this record of my sense of waste now fills me

with nostalgia: I survived it. When I returned to Illinois last year my friend Julia was astonished that it didn't depress me. "I thought the memories might be too painful," she said. I thought about this. And I told her: no, because it worked. If I had given up and gone back, then I would have to have thought of that period in Illinois as "the time when I was crazy." But however awful it was, I went through and out the other side. And rereading what I felt then, I look back liking myself for the guts that felt so gutless, whereas I look back on myself in times of strength judgmentally, see myself as pushy, overconfident, full of illusion. Is this a good thing? A sort of balance? Merely inevitable?

It is almost exactly six years since I drove down from the stop-gap job in Illinois to take up as an associate professor at Florida State. The boys with Walter in Champaign and I alone on the road—the Big White American Woman in the Big White American Car—I felt lost in space. Nobody knew where I was. I did not know where I was. Between Birmingham and Montgomery, those violent towns, I picked up two girl hitchhikers for the company, then heard their redneck violence as my short future, waited to see them take pistols from their white vinyl purses.

Carefully, on arrival in Tallahassee, I reminded myself that I had come to love places that I hated as much as I hated this one. Clearly I did not believe it. The asphalt outside the window of the La Jacaranda apartments sickened me. I could not write with a view of painted parking lines on graveled asphalt. I wanted to go *home!* And believed that I would never have a home again.

Here, in the house that *Raw Silk* built, I can see from my den window, and have done so for two years: hyacinths, azaleas, pine, palm, pecan, oak, dogwood, gardenia, ivy, camellias, honeysuckle, wisteria, and figs that are nearly ripe. On the feeder over my head outside, the black-capped chickadees strew seed at me; the tufted nuthatchers, cardinals, jays, two doves, and one woodpecker squabble at each other and at my typewriter.

Several days ago I recorded that I had 21 pages of *Opening Nights*. Today I do not know how many I have, and I suspect it is little better than two-thirds of that. What I have is no good. But something is happening.

MURIEL RUKEYSER

The Education of a Poet

This essay is adapted from a talk given under the auspices of
the Academy of American Poets in December 1976.

I was born in New York, in the house where a famous gangster
lived, beside Grant's Tomb, very near the grave of the Amiable
Child, at that corner of the Hudson River. And the life, both
open and masked, first of the people of the city, and of the
country, and of the world, opened itself to me. One opens,
yes, and one's life keeps opening, and poets have always known
that one's education has no edges, has no end, is not separated
out and cannot be separated out in any way, and is full of
strength because one refuses to have it separated out.

One wanted to be for the things of the world, and the way
that they came to a young child, to a girl, to me, went like
this: the excitement of the city and the excitements of my
family, who came to this city from other places, these were

very very strong. I came later to think that my whole generation, all my friends, thought that their imagination and fantasies were much stronger than their parents'. As we went on, we came to see that the imagination of our parents, however far underground, was strong and wild and fierce, and was acted out in history as well as in their private lives.

The child that I was then had nothing to do with the poetry of books. The poetry at home was only that of Shakespeare and the Bible. There were no books in the beginning. Later, there were the sets that were laughed at as pieces of furniture bought neither with discrimination nor taste. But these can also be seen in quite a different way, as the entire works of writers about whom one came to care. And so I was exposed to Dickens, Dumas, Victor Hugo, de Maupassant, Balzac. There was the Britannica, there was the Book of Knowledge, and My Book House, and Journeys Through Bookland. The popular history of art was there, as well as the popular history of science, and with the beginnings of science came the beginnings of pictures of nakedness. Nakedness was not shown at home. A great deal was done in secrecy, without open talk. There were three things that were never talked about: sex and money and death. They were taboo, and those giant taboos were powerful. The line that was on the wall beside my bed began "Where did you come from," and whether or not I was "Baby Dear" (and pretty soon I knew I wasn't), the "where did you come from" was very very strong.

We apartment children lived as gangs, with each gang set against every other, building by building all the way around the square block. There were the heroes: Ted Lewis, who lived in our house and asked "Is everybody happy?" and we didn't answer. There was Albert Payson Terhune and the collie Lassie who became the dog of our culture. D. H. Lawrence lived a block away at that time, but we didn't know that. When we could cross the street, we ran down the block to a certain window where the baseball scores would be held out on that art material used by everybody: the cardboards that came back from the laundry with the shirts. We would draw on them and write down the baseball scores, and discuss the exploits of heroes like Walter Johnson.

Form came in these ways. Form came in with the games, and a little later with golf, which had its own form and which technically one had to learn to perfection. I was expected to grow up and become a golfer. At a certain point, I stopped cold and never played again. But that was what I was supposed to be—a bridge-playing, golf-playing woman who if I wanted to write (and it was quite clear that I did) could write if I would do things that would let me write in the summer, teaching for instance. Or, it was suggested to me in my adolescence, it would be a good idea if I married a doctor, and when he was out on housecalls I could write my poems. Now of course we have no housecalls and we have women poets—the culture has changed to that extent.

But the preparation for poetry was strong. It was partly the silences of the house and the extreme excitement of the family. It was a building-business family, and the building was the building of New York. The method was the pouring of concrete, concrete that became the means of building—not the construction with stone and brick, but with the prestress concrete that involves a skeleton of metal. The riveters on those skeletons, and the throwing of redhot rivets, and the acrobatics and heroics impressed me, as did the pouring of concrete and that other use of form, the concrete being poured into forms.

My father was a young cement salesman who somehow got

a chance at a sand quarry on Long Island. He needed somebody with a horse and wagon. He was given an introduction to a young Italian who lived in Jersey City. Together my father and the young, thin Generoso Pope formed a sand and gravel company, and the trucks of that company went around the city with their concrete mixers turning. The company never needed any advertising because those machines were the ads.

To a child, to a little girl whose family was coming up with the building of New York and who felt the astonishing ambition and pride that went with the building, to that child the pouring and its terms became part of life. I remember being scolded in school when I said "orange peel crane," a technical term so obscure that nobody could possibly understand it. I remember being asked what grit was, and I said "number 4 gravel" when I was supposed to say "courage."

There were these things, and there were the questions of love and hate. The terrible silences among my mother, my father, and my much-loved aunt, my mother's older sister. They would have hot, passionate quarrels—forbidden times as far as I was concerned. Once I was prevailed upon to copy "Love's Old Sweet Song" and send it to my aunt so that she would talk to my mother again, and so that my father could see her again. This forbidden love was something that ran beneath the entire life of the family and went on and on until, just after my mother's death, my father married that aunt. Then, when they were in their late seventies, the whole relationship exploded into the cruelty and passion toward which it had been heading all along.

As a child I was not allowed to go across the street, and at one point my friends made a ring around me and pulled me across the street while I shouted, "But I promised I wouldn't cross." A promise was always unbreakable. It was through a promise that I knew really what writing poems meant to me. That didn't come until high school when my best friend said she wouldn't talk to me unless I would stop writing poems. I had to *promise* to stop writing. Not being talked to was the worst punishment I could imagine; I gave my promise at once. For four weeks I didn't question; it wasn't anything I would question. And then a poem began. I went into a great storm about that poem which was building and forming. I lived like that for two weeks, and finally one night I got up and wrote down the poem. At school the next morning I said to that friend, "I couldn't keep my promise," and she said "What promise?" I realized in a flash that it meant nothing to her and I knew what it meant to me. The pressure and the drivenness was in that moment, and has been there ever since.

The punishment of silence also came at home. Home was an apartment building on the West Side. The cellars of these buildings were places that the children made their own, and the roofs, and the sidewalks, and Riverside Drive, and the river itself. The river was quite different in those days. It was openly brutal: the cattle trains came down in the morning, and you could see the cattle going to the slaughterhouses; you could smell them. The whole city was open; the railroad tracks were not covered. Beyond the tracks was a place called Shanty-town and, later, Hooverville. The people in the fine apartment houses insisted that Hooverville be destroyed because it spoiled their view. It was clear to a growing child that the terrible, murderous differences between the ways people lived were being upheld all over the city, that if you moved one block in any direction you would find an entirely different order of life. One morning I missed walking with my father to the car that took him to his office, which was on the edge of the river and the sandhills at Fiftieth Street. I went after him, and as I walked the neighborhood changed; the apartment houses and the residential blocks changed to the poor blocks with the smell of the poor, the smell of barley, the open doorways, the people lying against walls, the people working, the metalworkers, and finally the offices of the sand and gravel company. These changes were the clear statement of what we were willing to live among, what we see still everyday, and these were the beginnings.

Friends were the beginnings too. The boy Rusty Shaw, who was a caddy at a country club. We used to lie on the hills of oyster shells at Inwood Bay, Long Island, and talk and talk about how he could possibly manage to go on living at home where his father was drunk all the time and took whatever money Rusty made. There were the people who understood about sex. Sex was never talked about; my hands had been bound up at night for good reason. I didn't know about sex until I walked with a girlfriend through the Museum of Natural History underneath the great whale, and she told me about sex. It is curious, and one can't say silly, the way one first hears about it, but there it was and I thought Ah, *that's* why my parents don't commit suicide! That seemed to be the thing that would save the life of people in such misery and such silence.

The *feeling* life of my parents seemed to me to be in the world of opera and music. They went to the opera on Thursday evenings, and on certain Friday mornings the libretto would be on the hall table. When I came home from school on Friday I would read it, and it seemed strange but no stranger than anything else. From the librettos, I first learned about translations, and about lurid poetry and melodrama. From melodrama, Caruso gave them the worship of emotion. It was the kind of emotion that did come through to my parents, even though a great deal of emotion was cut off for reasons that I didn't know about then. Much later I read Jung, and when I went to Ireland I heard about an analyst who believed that what you are dominated by in your childhood is whatever your parents really love. I believe that now. I believe that I was dominated by what my father and my mother loved; it came through to me as deep sexuality centered in that forbidden aunt who was the figure of passion and sex in my early life, and through the opera singers and composers of the music that meant so much to them, and through the popular music of that time and the happiness of the young people who sat on the stoops and sang, and through the sadness my parents felt at that custom going out of the city.

I was beginning to write poems, and also to make up short piano pieces. But I didn't know what writing meant to me until that promise I gave in high school. The drivenness, the fact that the writing has to be done beyond all promises was there for a long time. There are promises to people one loves that take precedence at times. But one can trust—one knows that the poetry will come back, that it will resurrect. It's a risky thing; the poetry may come back on a different level. But it will come back. It came back to me. I never put it away completely. I was told by friends, for example, when it was a matter of deciding to go ahead and have a child, that I would have to choose between the child and poetry, and I said no. I was not going to make that choice; I would choose both.

It's very much a question of reinforcing choices as one makes them, of leaving one's life open to them, of going further in and confirming them, and also of clearing away, stripping away the masks. I said earlier that we thought that our imaginations were so much stronger than our parents', but I think that idea came from our not knowing how people with masked lives really lived. These were middle-class lives. There was no idea at that point of a girl growing up to write poems. That was a terrifying idea to my parents. Much later they said they thought they could have handled it if I had been a boy, but they were very strange in their feeling about anybody writing poems or doing anything serious in the arts.

How old were you when you know that there were living poets? Do you remember? In this culture a great many people don't know that there are living poets, or didn't know when I was growing up. I thought that real men went to the office everyday. The joy of learning that people wrote poems and that was what they could do with their lives was very great. I came to that knowledge through anthologies and single books of poems and through poets' collected poems, the fact that one could find the whole work of a person in one book and see how that spirit moves. I want to share with you some poems of mine, poems that have to do with the way my life has taken its shape.

THE RETURN

An Idea ran about the world
screaming with the pain of the mind
until it met a child
who stopped it with a word.

The Idea leaned over those newborn eyes
and dreamed of the nature of things:
the nature of memory and the nature of love;
and forgave itself and all men.

Quieted in a sea of sleeping
the Idea began its long return—

renewed by the child's sea-colored eyes
remembered the flesh, smiled and said:

I see birds, spring and the birthplace
unknown by the stable stone.
I know light and I know motion
and I remember I am not alone.

The Idea voyaged nearer my breathing, saying
Come balance come
into the love of these faces and forces
find us our equilibrium.

And the child stirred, asking his questions.
The Idea grew more fleshly and spoke:
Beaten down I was
Down I knew very long
Newborn I begin.

And the child went on asking his questions.

The Idea journeying into my body
returned, and I knew the nature of One,
and could forget One, and turn to the child,
and whole could turn to the world again.

Until the pain turns into answers
And all the masters become askers
And all the victims again doers
And all the sources break in light.

The child goes alive, asking his questions.

The Education of a Poet   225

There are the questions of love and religion that have to enter, along with the social bonds between us, into everything we do. My mother had a story about recovery from illness that was central to her life. As she told the story, it went like this: "My mother was a heroic and noble woman. She saved my life. When I had diphtheria as a child and they gave me up for dead, she stayed all night feeding me cracked ice. By morning the fever had broken. If she hadn't fed me that ice all night long, I would never have come through." My mother also gave me a treasure that I believe has a great deal to do with the kind of poetry I think of as unverifiable fact. She told me we were descended from Akiba. Akiba was the martyr who resisted the Romans in the first century and who was tortured to death after his great work for the Song of Songs. He was flayed with iron rakes tearing his flesh until at the end he said, "I know that I have loved God with all my heart and all my soul, and now I know that I love Him with all my life." Now this is an extraordinary gift to give a child.

I've always thought of two kinds of poems: the poems of unverifiable facts, based in dreams, in sex, in everything that can be given to other people only through the skill and strength by which it is given; and the other kind being the document, the poem that rests on material evidence. So many parts of life have come into my poems. One recent poem that has formed over several years is called "Double Ode." I didn't know fully what the poem was when I began it. I thought it was a poem in which the figures of father and mother were represented both by the remembered parents and also by two small black Mexican statues that are on my windowsill. But as I went on with the poem, pieces came into it from my notebooks, pieces from Spain, from the bells in the towers of Florence, from the exile of my son and daughter-in-law during the Vietnam War. I realized that the doubleness of the ode was the doubleness of looking backwards and forwards, that it was not simply a poem of parents but of generations.

I need to speak also of my formal education, because at college everything was sharply intensified. I could spend long times in the library, I could take to bed for days, and I could also go to the coal mines in Pennsylvania (although when my parents came up and I said, "Do you want to go for a drive?" My mother said, "You mean the gate isn't locked? I never would have let you come here if I thought the gate wasn't locked.") There was so much more freedom, and an access to materials and to people who were more than I had thought people could be. It was there that everything opened again, but I left college because my father had gone bankrupt and could not afford to have a daughter at Vassar. I went ahead writing poems, the poems that were in my first book. It was a piece of luck that my first book was published, and an act of extreme generosity on the part of the editor of the Yale Series of Younger Poets. I sent my book in partly finished form the same year that James Agee's book entered the competition. Stephen Vincent Benet, the editor, wrote me that he'd had to choose between Jim Agee's book and mine, and he had chosen Jim's. He thought that my book could be published by a commercial firm, and he gave me letters of introduction. My book was turned down by eleven publishers during that year, and finally Benet asked me to put the book back in the Yale Series, saying of course it would have to stand in the competition. But he did publish it that year. A great deal of my life has involved that preliminary "no" and a final "yes," and I felt very lucky.

I could go on for days and talk about my entire life, but what I've begun to say here shows the direction, the strength of the poetry itself. I don't believe that poetry can save the world. I do believe that the forces in our wish to share something of our experience by turning it into something and giving it to somebody: that is poetry. That is some kind of saving thing, and as far as my life is concerned, poetry has saved me again and again. I don't know a lot of things. This year a friend asked me what direction my work was taking. I blurted out, as I do, and said I didn't know. I asked him if he knew where his work was taking him and he said yes, that it was going in a certain direction—socially, always. And for him that was one part and the other part was a mystery. I wish I had given that answer. I give it to you, and a poem as well:

RECOVERING
Dream of the world
speaking to me.

The dream of the dead
acted out in me.

The fathers shouting
across their blue gulf.

A storm in each word,
an incomplete universe.

Lightning in brain,
slow-time recovery.

In the light of October
things emerge clear.

The force of looking
returns to my eyes.

Darkness arrives
splitting the mind open.

Something again
is beginning to be born.

A dance is
dancing me.

I wake in the dark.

People have said that we contemporary poets are writing
without form. I was brought up with forms and care very
much about them. I care about the form in which the poems in
the Bible are written, its parallelism that allows one to make
one's own synthesis of whatever meanings one derives from op-
posites. But the idea that form has to be the forms of the past
is nonsense. I was startled to read of Thurber's anger when he
found out that the world wasn't necessarily round, that it
might be pear-shaped. He said he couldn't stand it, he wanted
to have form. I'd be very happy with the form of a pear. In
order to give something to somebody there must be the form
to shape the experience. It's difficult to make the equivalent of
an experience, to make a poem that is so full of the resources of
music and of meaning, and that allows you to give it to me,
me to give it to you. All the forms of art come to us in their
own ways and allow us to make more forms, and to make this
exchange. I used to talk a great deal about communication. I
don't anymore. I communicated badly with the people I was

closest to, so I won't talk about it any longer. I'll try to do it. I
think the exchange of energy is what happens in art. There are
so many ways in which one is conducted to learning, so many
ways in which one seeks, and ways in which one loves the people from whom one can learn. The passion with which one
reaches to such people goes on forever and ever; it is in one's
poems, and in the poems one reads, and in this poem:

THEN

When I am dead, even then,
I will still love you, I will wait in these poems,
When I am dead, even then
I am still listening to you.
I will still be making poems for you
out of silence;
silence will be falling into that silence,
it is building music.

GAIL GODWIN

Becoming a Writer

On weekend mornings my mother sat at the typewriter in a sunny breakfast nook and wrote stories about women, young women like herself, who, after some difficulty necessary to the plot, got their men. In the adjoining kitchen, my grandmother washed the breakfast dishes and kept asking, "What do you two think you could eat for lunch?" My mother and I would groan in unison. Who could imagine lunch when we'd just finished breakfast? Besides, there were more important things to do than eat.

Already, at five, I had allied myself with the typewriter rather than the stove. The person at the stove usually had the thankless task of fueling. Whereas, if you were faithful to your vision at the typewriter, by lunchtime you could make two more characters happy—even if you weren't so happy yourself. What is more, if you retyped your story neatly in the afternoon and sent it off in a manila envelope to New York, you'd get a check back for $100 within two or three weeks (300 words to the page, 16–17 pages, 2¢ a word: in 1942, $100 went a long way). Meanwhile, she at the stove ran our mundane life. Still new to the outrageous vulnerability of widowhood, she was glad to play Martha to my mother's Mary. In our manless little family, she also played mother and could be counted on to cook, sew on buttons, polish the piano, and give encouragement to creative endeavors. She was my mother's first reader, while the stories were still in their morning draft; "It moves a little slowly here," she'd say, or "I didn't understand why the girl did this." And the tempo would be stepped up, the heroine's ambiguous action sharpened in the afternoon draft; for if my grandmother didn't follow tempo and motive, how would all those other women who would buy the magazines?

To my grandmother's mother, my mother played father; she was the provider, who took her skills off to the next town on the weekday bus and returned home at night, rumpled and exhausted and as in need of being waited on as any man. Lucky for her, most of the men were overseas at war, and the *Asheville Citizen-Times* needed reporters. Out she went daily; at the new Army hospital, she interviewed wounded soldiers who had flown back home; she followed Eleanor Roosevelt all over town one day and bore the brunt of the restaurant owner's ire when Mrs. R. insisted upon bringing her black friend to lunch; she interviewed Béla Bartók in her college French; whenever Mrs. Wolfe called up the paper to announce, "I have just remembered something else about Tom," my mother was sent off immediately to the dead novelist's home on Spruce Street. It was not uncommon, during blackouts, for my mother to arrive home via police escort; they at the *Citizen* did not think it proper that a young woman should be alone in all that darkness; but the other side of this special treatment was that, after the war, she was told her skills would not be needed anymore. "The men need their jobs back, you see."

My preschool occupation consisted of being the adored Child on whose behalf this family had been created. For if I had not existed, these two might have worked out different plots for themselves. My elegant, feminine grandmother, doted on by men who wanted to protect her, would not have remained long on her own. My mother was still young, pretty as any of the girls who stepped off trains or entered fateful rooms in her stories; she had a master's degree in English ("The Stage of Inigo Jones": her thesis); an only child, she had been brought up in comfort, riding around the country on passes—her father was with Southern Railways—shopping almost daily for clothes from the moment she could walk with her mother (I can open her college diary today and read about the rose silk pajamas they bought, or the yellow taffeta tea gown, and what movie they saw afterward) and I know (also from the diary) that in the years just before me her main problem had been choosing between men. At Chapel Hill, she often had five dates in one day—and the energy of the true candle-burner-at-both-ends; she thought nothing of staying up during what was left of the night, typing nineteen-page term papers, or writing her own plays. But at home one weekend, she was playing bridge with her girlfriends on the porch when a man limped by. It was Mose Winston Godwin, the handsome local bachelor, who had snapped his ankle playing tennis. My mother's little dog, incensed by something in the man's gait, rushed down the stairs and bit his good leg.

And that was that. Sealed. My mother's fate. And mine.

GIRL MEETS MAN. MUTUAL ATTRACTION. THINGS DEVELOP. A PROBLEM ARISES. CONFLICT AND DOUBT. RESOLUTION OF CONFLICT. FINAL EMBRACE. The formula was unvarying. All the stories that bought my clothes, my storybook dolls, my subscriptions to children's magazines, were contained by, were imprisoned in that plot. Did my young divorced mother, while typing in that sun-filled breakfast nook, ever have moments of bitter irony when she was tempted to rip out the "happily ever after" lie she was perpetrating, and roll a fresh sheet into the carriage and tell her own story? It would have been much more interesting. But who would have bought it? Not *Love Short Stories,* nor any of the other pulps—nor any of the "slicks" for women, either. When you write for the market, you lock yourself willingly into the prison of your times: a lesson I learned early. Now I sit in my dentist's office and leaf through women's magazines whose fictional terrains support, quite matter-of-factly, divorced mothers, unmarried mothers, even well-to-do suburban wives who may or may not "keep" that unplanned-for last child. And I think of the writers of these stories, safely within the ideologies of their *zeitgeist,* and I wonder what parts of their own stories they still feel obliged to suppress, what dark blossomings of their imaginations still lie outside the realm of the current "market"? Yes, even in these "liberated" times.

It is this realm that I fight; it is the dark blossomings, the suppressed (or veiled) truths that I court. Not always successfully. Like my mother, I, too, am the child of my times.

Here is a story that my mother did not write: a woman, coming home late from her creative writing class, walks past the Casa Loma nightclub, on the way to her bus stop. She sees a man go in, a handsome, laughing, well-dressed man with his arm around a platinum blonde. Upstairs in the nightclub, the band is in the throes of "Stardust." The woman downstairs in the night, alone, has been up since six that morning, teaching at two schools, teaching, among other things, Romantic Literature. She has been unable to collect a single child-support payment from the handsome man because he has moved to another state. But now he has sneaked back into this town, unable to resist his old haunts. He has not seen the woman in the rumpled tweed suit, downstairs in the night. An irresistible impulse rises in her. She goes to the nearest phone and calls the police and identifies herself. They remember her, from her wartime job at the paper; many of them have taken turns driving her home during the old blackouts. She has my father locked up. She misses her bus but boards the next one and rides through the starry night, a weird joy throbbing through her veins and making her feel lightheaded. When she arrives home, she gives in to another irresistible impulse and wakes her little girl. "It's almost midnight," cries the grandmother, "are you crazy?" "No," she says, smiling. She hugs them both. She will keep her secret for tonight, as it will just upset her mother, who fears scandal as much as disease. "I want Gail to see the stars," she says. "They have never seemed quite so close."

But if the next day was Saturday, her "free day," she probably sat down and fabricated yet another fortuitous beginning. Girl would meet man, at work, at a party, on a trip. (A biting dog would create the wrong tone.) And once set on her romantic treadmill, she has only to stand in place—or even sit—and let her author make it happen for her: the mutual attraction, the developing passion, the necessary conflict, the happy ending. The final embrace is a blind one, containing no foreknowledge of difficulties, no intimation of separation or sorrow—and certainly not the sort of retributive prank against one's former beloved that would send a weird joy pumping through one's veins.

My mother's specialty was the representative heroine, not the singular, the "passing strange." For practical reasons, she must keep editing the most interesting parts of herself out of the heroines she sent to New York. To explore all those oddities and promptings that rustled like wings in her soul at night, while she—who longed to write a love scene as it really was—lay beside her small daughter? Ah, better not, better not. For practical reasons, for reasons of sanity as well.

"Your mother always did have a sense of humor. Not that I felt much like laughing that night they came and hauled me out of the Casa Loma. But, do you know, you can get the best view of Asheville from its jail? All those ranges and ranges of blue mountains cradling the town. Especially when it's lit up at night. By the time your Uncle William came to bail me out, I had organized the other prisoners into a clean-up squad. They were nice fellows, just a little beleaguered, that was all. We were going to wash down the walls and then whitewash them over." My father laughed, thirteen years after the fact, a few months before his own suicide. "I was sort of sorry to have to leave. It was an interesting experience, being in jail."

Fact and fiction: fiction and fact. Which stops where, and how much to put in of each? At what point does regurgitated autobiography graduate into memory shaped by art? How do you know when to stop telling it as it is, or was, and make it into what it ought to be—or what would make a better story?

Choices, choices.

The child of two women, I sat down to write my first story

at age nine. What was the story about? A henpecked husband named Ollie McGonnigle, who insults a man one morning only to come home that evening and discover that his wife has invited that same man to dinner. And, moreover, that man is—THE MAYOR OF THE TOWN!

My mother remarried. One of her ex-GI students from her Romantic Literature class. She wrote a novel about a college teacher, courted by several veterans, each of whom had a story to tell about his life and about the war. The teacher marries one of the veterans. This novel, called, *And Not to Yield,* contained, to my memory, some of the most erotic love scenes I have ever read. Amazing, when you think of it: the sheltered little girl and her grandmother, sitting down each evening to read the next installment of *And Not To Yield.* It was fiction, of course. My grandmother had not approved of the new groom, but this book was interesting. Hmmm. "Your mother certainly knows how to keep a reader's interest," my grandmother said, moistening her thumb to turn the page. "Kathleen Cole writes like an angel," wrote the publisher to my mother's agent, "at times. At other times, she is much too facile . . . and sentimental."

I went to a private school run by a French order of nuns. I was the poorest girl in the class, the only one who could not fork up the twenty-five dollars for the eighth grade trip to Washington. What story did I write in those days? One about a little rich boy, who lived all day behind elegant iron gates and had everything he wanted—except a friend he could confide in.

My mother miscarried her first son. Her husband got a job as a management trainee at Kress, for forty-five dollars a week. A courtly older man in town, the renowned local portrait painter (also the teacher of my mother's former creative writing class), painted my mother's portrait in oils. In the portrait she wore a jade green silk blouse and a gold Chinese pin. She also wore an enigmatic smile. She started a new novel about a famous woman writer, with two men after her. One, her ex-husband, was now her literary agent, who always leveled with her about her work. The other was a celebrated portrait painter. She also had a daughter, "pretty but selfish." The daughter got to marry the boy she loved: the son of the painter. The portrait painter, who has been looking for the "perfect woman" to paint, chooses another woman in town, a less beautiful but selfless woman who has been a wonderful mother. At the end of the novel, the successful writer-heroine is told by her ex-husband that her writing has become too facile and shallow. Having lost both the portrait painter and her writing, she turns to religion. When she has chastened herself sufficiently, she remarries her ex-husband. This novel was called *The Everlasting Door*. It went the round of the publishers. Take out the religion, some publishers said. Take out the sex, said others, and maybe a religious house would be interested.

Begin again.

My mother had a baby girl. I was fifteen and fell in love with an athlete nobody approved of but me. But we were going to move from that town soon, to Norfolk. Kress moved my stepfather often, and what I wanted to do more than anything was "stay out all night" with Larry. So I lied, and did. We didn't "do" anything, of course: it was 1953, and it had been drummed into me often enough what my most valuable commodity was. But the girl I was supposed to be spending the night with "told," and I was disgraced. I lost all my friends the same week I moved from that little South Carolina town. In Norfolk, we knew not one soul. There was a whole summer ahead of me in which to smolder over the injustice of society. I borrowed my mother's typewriter in the hours she wasn't using it and wrote a short novel called *I Broke the Code*. I have this piece of work before me now. An interesting artifact. Part truth, part lie, part gauche attempt at craft ("True, some will believe the worst, but I like to think that every small town has a forgiving streak that crosses right down its center like the railroad tracks.") and part cliché ("A wave of shame rushed through me."). Pretty disgusted with the results, I condescended and sent it to *True Confessions,* who returned it with the reader's note clipped to the top: "Some good writing but overdone. Also *much* too long. Also nothing much happens."

My mother had another miscarriage in Norfolk. Like me, she had no friends yet. So she organized a local Toastmistress Club, her civic specialty, begun back in Asheville when, after hearing a Red Cross volunteer open her speech with, "Ladies, our deficit is astounding," my mother decided it indeed was, and that women should do better than this. Now Norfolk women flocked to learn how to organize their thoughts and project their voices before crowds. My mother was gratified; her spunk returned. "Oh, what the hell," she said. "I am going to sit down and write a dirty novel that will really sell." *The Otherwise Virgins* was set on a college campus in the South. It had three heroines: Debby, a poised and beautiful redhead, president of her sorority, who unbeknownst to her friends was formerly a callgirl in New York until a southern senator decided to adopt her and give her a new start; Lisa, a dark-haired freshman, also beautiful, but spoiled and determined to win the love of Mark, an ex-GI just returned to campus; and Jane, a minister's daughter, a shy and scholarly girl, who joins Debby's sorority and rooms with Lisa. Complications arise when Mark discovers Debby on campus. He remembers her from her other life. They had a night together before he shipped out with his regiment for France. Further complications arise when Jane discovers she is a lesbian and deeply loves her roommate, Lisa.

I loved that novel. What excitement, during those dreary summer days in Norfolk when we knew nobody, to read each new page as it came out of the typewriter. My mother sometimes wrote twenty pages a day; a compulsion came over her during novels, it drove her to the end. Unlike me today, she always wrote with the completion taken for granted. It never occurred to her that she might get stuck, might not finish. She had always finished her stories for the old wartime pulps—unfinished stories didn't sell. A photographer from the Norfolk paper came and took my mother's picture at the typewriter, flanked by her sixteen-year-old daughter and her seven-month-old daughter. "Mrs. Cole writes novels and starts toastmistress clubs in her spare time," the captions read.

"*The Otherwise Virgins* has come heartbreakingly close," wrote the agent, many months and submissions later. "What the publishers seem to feel is that this novel is neither fish nor fowl. The campus life is realistic, but the situation is implausible. Also the World War II background is dated. Perhaps if you made it the Korean War and took out the part about the Southern senator . . ."

But if she took out the southern senator, she must take out Debby's past life, and if she took that out, there went the plot. And the Korean War had only ended the year before. Besides, we were moving again, across the river to Portsmouth. My mother consoled herself by starting another Toastmistress Club.

The writing bug did not bite again until a year later. We had been talking about my father and whether I should invite him to my high school graduation. She sat down and wrote a story about a selfish playboy father who suddenly takes an interest in his seventeen-year-old daughter, whom he has not seen for years. He invites her to come and live with him in his sumptuous house. ("Keep it," his rich second wife had said. "I never had a happy moment in it.") The girl goes, but ends up being more of an opportunist than he. She abandons him after two months when the rich ex-wife offers to send her to art school. "Nothing is going to stop me from reaching my goal," the daughter writes in her farewell note which she leaves with his housekeeper. "Maybe you're thinking I am ungrateful. But really, these two months have been so little in comparison with all you could have given me in seventeen years." She has even taken the curtains and bedspreads from her room.

"I'm not that bad, am I?" I asked.

"Of course not, darling. You're ambitious, like she is, but you would never have taken the curtains. I've brought you up better. But I needed her to be as ruthless as she is because I wanted this story to have that fated circular shape, like Greek drama."

Twenty years later, my mother, my sister, and I sat in my sister's girlhood bedroom, talking about a novel I had written. "I don't care," Franchelle was saying. "She'd better never put me in a novel again. I don't like being frozen in print for the rest of my life, forever wearing those silly panties and short skirts; and I'm *not* big like that, she's made me into some sort of amazon-freak."

"Darling," our mother said, "the sister in *The Odd Woman* wasn't you. Gail just took parts of you, the parts she needed. Writers work that way."

"Well, I wouldn't know. I'm a lawyer and they don't work that way. Besides, it *hurts.*"

Tears filled her eyes and she ran from the room.

Becoming a Writer   241

"It's unfair," I said, "She's being unfair by not trying to understand."

"It's difficult when you haven't written," agreed my mother. "Now I understood why you had to make Kitty a more passive mother than I am, also a little stupid; that was necessary to your overall plan . . ."

"Passive! Stupid! Kitty? Kitty was a beautiful character. I worked hard on Kitty."

"She was a lovely character," my mother said. "I thought she was awfully well done. But what I mean is, I knew she wasn't supposed to be me."

"But she was!"

"Well, there was something left out, then."

The magazines rejected my mother's story about the father and daughter. "Well-written, but there are no sympathetic characters," wrote one editor.

My father floored everyone by showing up for my high school graduation. He had to introduce himself, as I had no idea who he was. I flung myself, weeping, into his arms and he invited me to come and live with him.

"It was a little scary," my mother told me a long time afterward. "I felt I had somehow made it happen by writing that story."

The house of the real father was not sumptuous, and his second wife (not rich) still lived in it with him. It was he, not she, who sent the ambitious daughter off to college. He could only afford the first year: his playboy days were over; he sold cars for his wife's brother-in-law. In real life, it was he, not the daughter, who left first. For some reason, he took off his watch and placed it on the bedside table. His wife returned from the grocery store and found him lying on the floor, but with his head off the rug to spare her the necesssity of dry cleaning it. He needn't have worried; it was a neat job. The coroner found that the first shot had misfired. So he had made his decision twice. There was no explanation, no farewell note to anyone. The daughter was in her third year of college, on a scholarship now. She was rewriting *The Otherwise Virgins*, updating the Chapel Hill campus her mother remembered from too long ago. Mark became a Korean War veteran, as it was now 1958 and there was plenty of information to look up on that war. "I give it to you," said her mother, now the mother of a little boy, too, and soon to be the mother of a second. "If you can do anything with it, you're welcome. I've somehow lost the urge." In her fourth year of college, the daughter would try and fail to complete a story about the father's death from the daughter's point of view. Many years later than that, she would finish an unsuccessful draft of a novel called *The Possibilitarian,* about a man of lost possibilities. Later again, her fourth published novel would contain a southern playboy uncle, Ambrose Clay, who shoots himself neatly in the head at the age of forty-nine because he has not kept his promises to himself. We know this is his reason because he leaves his niece, a young painter who will be warned by his failure and pursue her promises because of it, a loving note. Like the real father, Ambrose at one point is a car salesman, but I made him sell Mercedes. Unlike the real father, Ambrose had wanted to be a good novelist—as the real mother had wanted.

Fact and fiction, fiction and fact. Shapeshifting into one another. Sometimes fact cries out for fiction; sometimes fiction cries out for yet another fiction. Sometimes fiction redeems fact. And sometimes it doesn't.

Miss Gail Godwin
The Miami Herald
Fort Lauderdale, Fla.

November___, 1959

Dear Miss Godwin:

Haven't I seen this novel before? You say you have just finished it, but I'm sure I recall the kindly southern senator and I'm sorry to say the plot is still as implausible as ever. Regretfully, I am shipping back *The Otherwise Virgins* to you under separate cover.

Sincerely yours,
Lurton Blassingame

Oh, Jesus, how could I have been so stupid? I thought my mother's agent was Ann Elmo. But obviously, at some point, she must have switched. Why can't I pay attention? What a stupid, self-defeating thing to do!

Failures often come in clumps. The next was the letter from my bureau chief.

August___, 1960

. . . I have spent more time working and worrying over your future than I have spent on the entire rest of the staff combined. I must confess I've been a failure. I apologize for my mistakes. But the fact remains that I cannot see any further benefit from my efforts or yours and I am convinced it would be to your benefit to find someplace to "start over." This has been harsher than I intended it to be. I really feel badly that I have failed to make a good reporter out of obviously promising material. I hope you can use this experience somewhere but I'm afraid you won't do it successfully until you look facts in the face and at the same time quit expecting to get to the moon in one day.

Failed! A failed writer, a failed journalist, at twenty-three. I don't know what to do. I'd rather die than tell my mother I was . . . fired. I'm afraid to kill myself, though. I don't have his nerve. I'll get married.

Divorced and twenty-four, I used the slow hours at my job at the U.S. embassy in London to work on my novel, *Gull Key,* about a young wife left alone all day on a Florida island while her husband slogs away at his job on the mainland. (He is a newspaper photographer.) Her discontent swells like a tidal wave . . . neighbors bicker and age and are held back by their children, making her wonder if marriage and motherhood are for her . . . a tryst with a sensitive man met in the art section of the public library provides the denouement, in which the husband "finds out" and his fist comes crashing through the glass door which she has locked against him and she bandages it up and they decide to separate. The final scene shows the heroine, chastened but re-energized, driving north on AIA, a modern Nora fleeing her doll's house in her own compact car. After a dozen English publishers turned it down, I sent it off to an agency I'd seen advertised in a magazine

WANTED: UNPUBLISHED NOVELS IN WHICH WOMEN'S PROBLEMS AND LOVE INTERESTS ARE PREDOMINANT. ATTRACTIVE TERMS.

Many months went by and no response. I called directory assistance. The agency had no phone. I went around to the address. It was an empty building. I had made only one copy of *Gull Key.*

The City Literary Institute was located in a cavernous old building in north London. Somebody said it had been a prison in Dickens's time. But once I discovered it, I attended it every Tuesday evening with the desperate faith of an afflicted person attending a religious shrine. I was badly in need of a miracle. I was twenty-seven years old and had not yet become what I had wanted to be since the age of five: a writer. True, I wrote every evening, long, exhaustive entries in my journal to compensate for my boring days. I had stayed for three years in my cushy government job—helping the British plan their holidays in the U.S.—when I had only intended to stay one year. I had begun countless stories and novels, but there was something "off" about all of them. Either they had the ring of self-consciousness about them, or else they started too slowly and petered out before I ever got to the interesting material that had inspired me in the first place, or else they were so close to the current problems of my own life that I couldn't gain the proper distance and perspective. I have the 1964 journal before me now. Following a long quote from John Updike, which begins, "Her face, released from the terrible tension of hope, had grown smooth. . . ." I have begun a story of my own:

> The knock on the bedroom door turned out to be, that Sunday morning, the knock of Richard's mother, instead of Richard.

This gets nowhere, after a page, and I begin again:

> She had not slept well the night before. Things had come to a premature crisis with her and Richard, and though he took her home with him every weekend she had begun to feel in the position of a rejected lover . . .

At this point, I become disgusted with fiction and impatient to record, for my eyes only, what the real situation was. I was trying to get a rugby player to propose to me. He cared for me, but his mother cared infinitely more.

> Andy's mother rushed into the room, sat down on the bed and hugged me. She smelled of violet water. She said, "I just can't lose you. I love you like a daughter. If you go back to America, I'll have to go, too. I just can't under-

stand it. It's sheer *stupidity* on his part. He'll lose you and then when rugby season is over he'll go crazy. He wrote to me this week, it was a lovely letter, he added up all your qualities, almost like 25% for this, 60% for that. Then he left a small reservation! As if you weren't a superwoman already! He said he'd never been so near the brink before, but that he needed time to see. I know he's going to fall for some faery doll of twenty. Or marry one of these English society types. If he can't rise to *this*! . . ."

Easy, in retrospect, to see the problems with the first two fictional openings. As well as the possibilities of the "real" opening. But in 1964, I could see neither and was in despair.

Our teacher at the City Literary Institute was an appealing woman who looked as though she had stepped out of another century. She wore her dark hair like Charlotte Brontë; her skirts were much too long for fashion. She had a rich, dramatically paced voice with which she read to us from the great writers. (When I reread Chekov's "Anyuta" recently, it seemed flat without Miss S——'s enthusiastic intonations and pregnant pauses.) But however she looked, our teacher was a thoroughly modern woman and somewhat of a heroine. She worked daytimes as an editor in a prominent publishing house, did interviews for the BBC on weekends, and taught these classes to support herself and her small illegitimate son. Miss S—— not only knew what good fiction was, she could tell you why it was good; she at once zeroed in on me, and, with a modicum of English tact, told me why my fiction wasn't working. That she was *able* to tell me, moreover to prescribe exercises to correct my faults, was my good fortune. What if I hadn't found my good angel, Miss S——? Later, when I was back in the U.S., and had become the writer I wanted to be, I tried to track her down through my English publishers, but to no avail. She seems to have vanished into thin air, she and her beautiful little boy, who would be almost a man by now. When I teach writing classes today I try to emulate her, try to match her standards.

The first exercise she gave me was: write a story of 200 words. Two hundred words is less than a typewritten page. Therefore it is necessary to get to the heart of the matter at once. What I had achieved accidentally in my journal entry about Andy's mother, I must learn to do on purpose.

Write a story of 300 words. Write a story of 450 words, beginning with this sentence: *"Run away," he muttered to himself, sitting up and biting his nails.*

When that must be your first sentence, it sort of excludes a story about a woman in her late twenties, adrift among the options of wifehood, career, vocation, a story that I had begun too many times already—both in fiction and reality—and could not resolve. My teacher wisely understood Gide's maxim for himself as writer: "The best means of learning to know oneself is seeking to understand others."

One of the exercises I like to give in writing courses is: imagine a person as much unlike yourself as possible; then write a scene, from that person's point of view, in which he/she is getting ready for bed.

At last the evening came when I was invited by Miss S—— to read my latest story aloud to the class. I was up to 4,500 words by then. The story was about an English vicar who has seen God, who writes a small book about his experience, and becomes famous. He gets caught up in the international lecture-tour circuit. My story shows him winding up his exhausting American tour at a small Episcopal college for women in the South. He is at his lowest point, having parroted back his own written words until he has lost touch with their meaning. He fears that, given the present pace and pressure of his public life, he will never again approach that private, meditative state of mind that brought God into focus in the first place.

Many drafts and two years later, this story, first titled "The Illumined Moment—and Consequences," later "An Intermediate Stop," would get me accepted into the Iowa Writer's Workshop. "She has some affectations, but we'll prune them," wrote the member of the reading committee on the bottom of my application.

A decade later than that, I was winding up my own exhausting reading tour in a fluorescent-lit classroom in Kansas City. It was an adult education course in Creative Writing. As I watched the members file in, many looking more exhausted than I felt, I wondered how I could manage to keep them awake for an hour. Beginning to panic, I leafed through the handsome leatherbound volume of my story collection, a Christmas gift from my publisher. All the stories I usually read—my "tour de force" stories—seemed much too long. Moreover, I had read some of them aloud so often that they were beginning to sound as if they had been written by somebody else. I suddenly lit on the vicar story, buried humbly among its flashier sisters, and it was like greeting an old friend who has known you "back when." I had never read this story aloud since its London debut, many a draft ago, in Miss S——'s class.

To fill in the time—for this group certainly deserved their hour's worth—I began by telling my audience the genesis of the story they were going to hear. Once I, too, had attended an evening class, like this one, after working all day at a job . . .

As I began to read them the story, my tiredness diminished; I could see them perk up, as well, for they were "in on" things. They were no longer "Gail Godwin the Visiting

Writer's Audience," they were people like me, on the same quest. With a wonderful jolt of recognition, I realized that my life was imitating the action of my vicar story, written all those years ago. For his resurgence came when, facing his last audience before the journey home, he turns his notecards, worn from too many previous lectures, face down on the rostrum. And standing before them, "a man like any other, no vision standing between them," he takes them into his confidence, gives them a guided tour of his English landscape, that private long-ago place where he had been granted his vision.

After I had read my story to Miss S———'s class, its most interesting member came up to me and pronounced himself pleased. Though he never turned in stories himself, he could be depended upon to deliver penetrating judgments upon the work of his classmates. His name was Dr. Marshall, and even the astute Miss S——— was a little in awe of him. He was a tall, dark, scowling man with a slight limp who came to class with a motorcycle helmet under his arm, often accompanied by a horsey-looking woman carrying a motorcycle helmet under her arm. Tonight, however, his companion had not come, and after we had discussed certain religious images in my story, he told me he was a psychotherapist. We discovered we lived on the same street in Chelsea, and he rode me home that evening on the back of his Vespa. Within two months we were married and I had time, as did my character Dane Empson, the American girl in *The Perfectionists,* to meditate amply upon the consequences of our impulsiveness. It had been, on both our parts, a "nervous attachment, rather than a sexual love," as D. H. Lawrence described the marriage of the couple in *St. Mawr,* a work I had the misfortune to discover *after* I became Mrs. Marshall. For one year, we did our best to drive each other crazy—and both almost succeeded. Our union finally dissolved a year later in a nightmarish vacation in Majorca; the figurative truths of that year, if not the literal ones, were to become my first published novel. But to give credit where it is due, this man who was impossible as my mate was the person who may well have made it possible for me to start being the writer I knew I had it in me to be. And I don't mean the obvious, that our marriage was to become the material for my novel.

As I have mentioned, he was a psychotherapist, and during our year together I saw him do wonders for several people. Some doctors are extraordinarily gifted as diagnosticians, and he was one of them; also, he was willing to try the most unorthodox of cures. This bothered me at the time; more conventional than I am now, I wanted him to declare himself a Jungian, a Freudian. Meanwhile, off he went to a scientology lecture, to see what useful ideas he could derive from that controversial organization. My own "cure," ironically, was derived from a method he had picked up from the scientologists. It consisted in asking the patient the same question over and over again until the patient comes up with an answer that sets off a feeling of "release" in him, a relieving certainty that he has at last *really* answered the question.

Shortly after our fiasco-vacation in Majorca, and just before I was to depart for the United States for a visit from which I suspect both of us unconsciously knew I would not return, we sat under a very old mulberry tree, which was staked and wired together to preserve it as long as possible. It was known locally as Sir Thomas More's mulberry, though that would have made it more than four hundred years old. The building where we lived was on the land that had once been his.

"I am going to die if I can't be a writer," I said.

"Why can't you be a writer?" he asked.

"Because . . . I don't know . . . something keeps getting in the way."

"I see. But why can't you be a writer?"

"Because! I told you, something never quite . . . jells."

"Hmm. But . . . why can't you be a writer?"

"Oh, I don't know. Look at my mother. She wrote and wrote and wrote. And nobody ever published her novels. Heartbreaking."

"Yes. But why can't *you* be a writer?"

"When I write in my journals, it's fine. You know it is, you bastard, you've read them yourself, without my permission. They flow, they're real. Whereas, the minute I put on my writing hat and sit down to 'write a story,' I bore myself to death. I kill it, I kill the whole thing."

"I see. Why can't you be a writer, then?"

"Because . . . because . . . OH, GOD! Because I'm afraid I might fail!"

The sun was weakening, cold for June, but I felt very warm, as if I'd been given an injection of some warm energy. "Good God," I said, "That's it! That's it, you know. What a spineless, lily-livered fraidy-cat I have been!"

"Yes, that's it," he said, in his cool professional voice. But I saw the blood come into his face: the blush of exhaltation: he knew he had freed me. Even if it meant freeing me from him.

In Iris Murdoch's novel *The Black Prince,* a writer says, "I live, I *live,* with an absolutely continuous sense of failure. I am always defeated, always. Every book is the wreck of a perfect idea. The years pass and one has only one life. If one has a thing at all one must do it and keep on and on and on trying to do it better."

I love that statement. Its stark pessimism is comforting. That statement expresses my feelings about my own work.

I work continuously within the shadow of failure. For every novel that makes it to my publisher's desk, there are at least five or six that died on the way. And even with the ones I do finish, I think of all the ways they might have been better. Rodin was right when he said that even an achieved work is never perfect; it is always susceptible to a modification that can make it better. But I believe that with enough practice and skill and good faith, you can learn to recognize when the work is achieved. There is such a thing as fussing too much; it can deaden the work. There is also such a thing as stopping too soon; this gives the work a kind of incompleteness that is more annoying than it is mysterious. Learning when "enough is enough" is the discipline of a lifetime. Perfection, however that ideal is measured, may not grace the work, but it should be sought during the process of the work.

I think the most serious danger to my writing is my predilection for shapeliness. How I love "that nice circular Greek shape" my mother spoke of; or a nice, neat conclusion, with all the edges tucked under. And this sometimes leads me to "wrap up" things, to force dramatic revelations at the expense of allowing the truth to reveal itself in slow, shy, and often problematical glimpses.

But my serious danger is also my strength. And so I must fight its temptations and preserve its rights at the same time. For it is the part of my talent that *selects* from what Henry James called "the rattle and the rumble" of ordinary existence, and fashions these literal happenings into another kind of truth called a story.

An example. That "story my mother didn't write." True,

she attended a creative writing class in the evening; and she held down several teaching jobs during the day. (Or was the creative writing class during that earlier time, when she still worked on the newspaper?) True, one evening, she spied my father, delinquent in his child-support payments, slipping up to the Casa Loma club. And true she had him locked up. And once, when I was still small enough to be picked up, she carried me outside in her arms to show me the stars. All the rest, including the weird joy she felt, is my interpretation. And the events that did happen did not all happen on the same night. That was my timing. What did I hope to gain by telling the story this way? Well, the night becomes the backdrop on which I glue five isolated events that add up to a certain truth about my mother's situation at that time.

But what about the *other* truths you lost by telling it that way? you ask.

Ah, my friend, that is my question, too. The choice is always a killing one. One option must die so that another may live. I do little murders in my workroom every day. I must commit some now, in order to bring this piece to a close.

This account of my own unfolding as a writer has been the truth. But it is also full of lies, many of which I'm not aware of. But in one sense, perhaps the most important, it is all true: it could have been written by nobody but me. What I have chosen to tell, how I have chosen to tell it, and what I have chosen not to tell, express me and the kind of writer I am.

I am my mother's child, weaned on shapely plots; the child of the woman who knew more about herself than she dared to put into her heroines.

I am the daughter of a man who, when locked up in prison, discovered it afforded the best view in town; who would whitewash the walls of the prison if he was forced to stay there; who would look back on prison after he was out of it and reflect on the interesting nature of the experience.

I am—thanks to the efforts of those who have loved me (and to some who have not) and thanks to the examples of people who did their work well, and thanks to the efforts of myself—my own woman.

I am haunted at this moment by what I may write next. The good thing about becoming older is that you gain time from that much more experience and can see where the real stories are. So many landscapes impose themselves upon the one I look out on as I write this. So many people present themselves before my inner eye, turning themselves this way and that, reminding me of their myriad aspects. I'm a novelist and a teller of tales, in a room alone, looking out on rain-washed grass, garden, trees, yet seeing as well a French chateau, a path in white rock in New Mexico, a dormitory room, a marriage bed. I'm watching a roomful of personalities parading their traits before me, giving me a fashion show, enticing me to buy. "I'm unique," says one. "So am I," says another. "I, too," says another. "Me, me!" cries a fourth. And all of them are right. Each of them is unique. And the more I write fiction, the more I want all of them. The more I understand: I am in all of them; all of them live in me.

I am also haunted by "the story I might not write." How I long to sneak into the future and snatch away the retrospect of one who could say: *"Oh yes, she wrote about this and this and this, while all the time, as close to her as her own skin, lay her real story, her true story, the whole story, the best story of all."*

What is that story?

Oh, you know-it-all daughterly ghost of myself, I am going to shake you within an inch of your life, I am going to wrestle with you all the rest of my days, I am going to employ all my tact and strength and wiles to force you to give up your secret!

Notes on Contributors

TONI CADE BAMBARA is the author of a novel, *The Salt Eaters,* and two collections of short stories, *Gorilla, My Love,* and *The Seabirds Are Still Alive and Other Stories.* She has also edited the anthologies *The Black Woman* and *Tales and Short Stories for Black Folks.* Her fiction and nonfiction has been translated into six languages. Trained as a dancer and an actress, she has worked with Katherine Dunham and the Etienne Decroux School of Mime in New York and Paris. A founding member of the Southern Collective of African-American Writers, she has taught black literature at universities throughout the country. A native New Yorker, she now lives in Atlanta, Georgia.

INGRID BENGIS is the author of *Combat in the Erogenous Zone,* which was nominated for a National Book Award in 1972. She has since published a novel, *I Have Come Here To Be Alone,* and is at work on a new novel.

JANET BURROWAY was born in Tucson, Arizona, in 1936 and was educated at Barnard College, Cambridge University, England, and the Yale School of Drama. She is the author of five novels, *Descend Again, The Dancer from the Dance, Eyes, The Buzzards,* and most recently, *Raw Silk.* She has also published two children's books, *The Truck on the Track* and *The Giant Jam Sandwich,* as well as a chapbook of her poetry and an adaptation from Latin. While living abroad, she wrote for British television and worked as a costume designer in England and in Belgium. She has taught at the University of Sussex, the Writer's Workshop at the University of Iowa, and is currently professor of English at Florida State University. She lives in Tallahassee with her husband and two sons.

JOAN DIDION was born in Sacramento, California, and graduated from the University of California at Berkeley. On winning first prize in the Vogue magazine Prix de Paris writing competition, she traveled east, worked at Vogue, and wrote her first novel, *Run River.* She has since returned to California and has published two other novels, *Play It As It Lays* and *A Book of Common Prayer,* as well as two collections of essays, *Slouching Towards Bethlehem* and most recently, *The White Album.* With her husband, John Gregory Dunne, she has written a number of screenplays, among them dramatizations of *Play It As It Lays, The Panic in Needle Park,* and *A Star Is Born.* She is currently at work on her new novel, *Angel Visits.*

GAIL GODWIN is the author of four novels, *The Perfectionists*, *Glass People*, *The Odd Woman* (nominated for the 1974 National Book Award) and *Violet Clay*, and a collection of stories, *Dream Children*. Her stories and essays have appeared in many periodicals, among them *Harper's*, *Esquire*, the *Atlantic*, *Redbook*, *Cosmopolitan*, *Mademoiselle* and *Ms*. She has written the librettos for four musical works by the composer Robert Starer: *The Last Lover*, *Apollonia*, *Journals of a Songmaker*, and *Anna Margarita's Will*. She has a B.A. in Journalism from the University of North Carolina and a PhD. in English from the University of Iowa, and has taught at the Writer's Workshop at the University of Iowa, Vassar College, and Columbia University. She has held National Endowment and Guggenheim Fellowships for fiction.

MARY GORDON was born in Far Rockaway, New York. She attended Barnard College and the Writing Program at Syracuse University. Her first novel, *Final Payments*, was nominated for the National Book Critics Circle award in 1978. Her short stories have been published in *Ms.*, *The Ladies' Home Journal*, *Mademoiselle*, *Virginia Quarterly Review*, and *Southern Review*. She lives in upstate New York, where she is completing a new novel.

SUSAN GRIFFIN is the author of several collections of poems, among them *Like the Iris of an Eye*. Her other published work includes a collection of stories, *The Sink*, as well as the prose books *Women and Nature*, *The Roaring Inside Her*, and *Rape: The Power of Consciousness*. Her play *Voices* was performed on public television, winning an Emmy in 1975; it has also been produced off-off-Broadway in a production directed by Estelle Parsons, and in theaters across the country and abroad. She has taught creative writing and women's studies at the University of California at Berkeley and at San Francisco State University. An active voice in lesbian feminism, she has completed a new book, *Pornography and Silence,* and is at work on a theatrical version of *Women and Nature.* She lives in Berkeley with her eleven-year-old daughter.

ERICA JONG is the author of four books of poetry, *Fruits & Vegetables* (1971), *Half-Lives* (1973), *Loveroot* (1975), and *At the Edge of the Body* (1979). She has also written two novels, *Fear of Flying* (1973) and *How To Save Your Own Life* (1977). As an essayist, she has contributed to a wide range of periodicals both here and abroad. A native New Yorker, she now lives in Connecticut with writer Jonathan Fast and a young daughter, Molly. Her new novel will be published this year.

MAXINE HONG KINGSTON was born in Stockton, California, in 1940. Her first book *The Woman Warrior: Memoirs of a Girlhood among Ghosts,* won the National Book Critics Circle award as the best book of nonfiction published in 1976. Her stories and essays have appeared in *The New York Times, Ms., The New Yorker, American Heritage,* and *New West.* She has completed her second book, *China Men.* A teacher of creative writing, she makes her home in Honolulu, Hawaii, with her husband, an actor.

NANCY MILFORD was born in Dearborn, Michigan, in 1938. She received her B.A. from the University of Michigan and her M.A. and Ph.D. from Columbia University. Her biography *Zelda* was first begun as her master's thesis and later was expanded into her doctoral dissertation. She has held a Guggenheim fellowship for biography. She serves on the boards of the Authors Guild, the Society of American Historians, and The Writers Room, of which she is a founding member. Currently she is at work on a biography of Edna St. Vincent Millay. She lives in New York City with her husband and three children.

HONOR MOORE graduated from Radcliffe College in 1967 and attended the Yale School of Drama. Her first play, *Mourning Pictures,* was originally performed at the Lenox Arts Center and has since been produced on Broadway and at regional theaters. A second play, *Years,* was performed in the Women's Project at the American Place Theatre in 1978. Her poems have been widely anthologized, and she has recently completed her first book-length collection. She is also the editor of *The New Women's Theatre: Ten Plays by Contemporary American Women* (1977). Currently she is working on *The Terry Project,* a theater piece adapted from the unpublished writings of a young schizophrenic woman.

MICHELE MURRAY was born Judith Michele Freedman in 1933 into a Jewish working-class family in Brooklyn. While attending American University, she converted to Roman Catholicism. She married writer James Murray and bore four children; with her family, she lived in Washington, D.C., and its suburbs. As a literary critic, her reviews appeared in such publications as *Commonweal, The New Republic, The National Observer,* and the *Washington Post.* The discovery at thirty-five that she had cancer impelled her to write four books before her death in 1974. One book for children, *Nellie Cameron,* was selected for the Junior Literary Guild; the other, *Crystal Nights,* was nominated for a Newberry Medal. Her anthology, *A House of Good Proportion: Images of Women in Literature,* was one of the first collections of its kind. Seven months after her death, her first book of poems, *The Great Mother,* was published. Her journals cover the years 1950 to 1974. From these volumes, Thomazine Shanahan, a writer who based her master's thesis on Murray's journals, has edited the selections in this book.

MURIEL RUKEYSER was born in 1913 and grew up in New York City. She is the author of more than a dozen volumes of poetry, among them *Theory of Flight* and *U.S.1,* and most recently *The Gates* and her *Collected Poems.* Her interest in science and its connection to art led her to write biographies of Willard Gibbs and Thomas Hariot; she has also written a prose study, *The Life of Poetry.* A lifelong activist for radical social change, she traveled to Spain during the Civil War, and fought against American involvement in Vietnam and against the spread of nuclear power. Among her many awards and honors are a Guggenheim Fellowship and the National Institute Award. Muriel Rukeyser died in February 1980.

JANET STERNBURG was born in Boston, Massachusetts, in 1943. A former filmmaker, she produced and directed films for national public television, among them *Virginia Woolf: The Moment Whole,* which won a Cine Golden Eagle Award, and *El Teatro Campesino,* which was featured at the New York Film Festival at Lincoln Center. Her poems, fiction, and essays have appeared in numerous magazines and anthologies, among them *The Best of '72, Aphra,* and *Ms.* She is co-author of a play based on the work of Louise Bogan, which has been broadcast on national radio. She has taught at the Wesleyan Writers Conference, in the Poets in the Schools program, and is currently on the graduate faculty of media studies at the New School. As director of Writers In Performance: the Poetry Series at the Manhattan Theatre Club, she conceives and stages poetry, fiction, and dramatic readings. She has completed her first collection of poems and is at work on a novel.

ANNE TYLER is the author of eight novels, among them *Earthly Possessions, Searching for Caleb,* and *A Slipping-down Life.* She was born in Minneapolis, Minnesota, in 1941, but grew up in Raleigh, North Carolina, and considers herself a southerner. She was graduated at nineteen from Duke University, where she twice won the Anne Flexner Award for creative writing. She has done graduate work in Russian studies at Columbia University and worked for a year as the Russian bibliographer at the Duke University Library. Her stories have appeared in many magazines, among them *The New Yorker* and *Harper's.* She is married to psychiatrist Taghi Mohammad Modaressi, and she and her husband now live in Baltimore, Maryland, with their two children.

ALICE WALKER was born in Georgia in 1944, attended Spelman College, and graduated from Sarah Lawrence College. She is the author of two books of poems, *Once,* and *Revolutionary Petunias.* A fiction writer as well, she has published *In Love & Trouble, Stories of Black Women,* and two novels, *The Third Life of Grange Copeland* (1970) and *Meridian* (1976). She has also published stories, poems, and essays in numerous magazines and anthologies. For many years she has taught courses in writing, black literature, and women writers. She has been a scholar at the Bread Loaf Writers' Conference and a fellow at the Radcliffe Institute. She has lived in Jackson, Mississippi, where she was actively involved in voter registration, and now lives in California with her young daughter.

MARGARET WALKER was born in Birmingham, Alabama, in 1915. She graduated from Northwestern University and received her master of arts from the University of Iowa, where her thesis was a book of poetry, *For My People,* which in 1942 won the Yale Award for Younger Poets. Her Civil War novel,

Jubilee, has been translated into seven languages; her other books are *Prophets for a New Day* (1970), *October Journey* (1973), and most recently *A Poetic Equation: Conversations between Nikki Giovanni and Margaret Walker.* Among her many honors are a Houghton Mifflin Literary Fellowship and a senior fellowship from the National Endowment for the Humanities. She has recently retired from Jackson State University where she was professor of English and director of the Institute for the Study of History, Life and Culture of Black People. She has completed a new volume of poems, *This Is My Century,* and is at work on a biography of Richard Wright.

Acknowledgments